In Search of Population Policy

VIEWS FROM THE DEVELOPING WORLD

A Report on Five Regional Seminars
Conducted in 1973 by
Office of the Foreign Secretary
Commission on International Relations
National Academy of Sciences–National Research Council
and
Cosponsoring Institutions in Developing Countries

NATIONAL ACADEMY OF SCIENCES   WASHINGTON, D.C.   1974

This report has been prepared by an international steering committee of the Office of the Foreign Secretary, National Academy of Sciences–National Research Council, for the Office of Population, Bureau for Population and Humanitarian Assistance, Agency for International Development, Washington, D.C., under contract No. AID/csd-3600.

Available from
Printing and Publishing Office, National Academy of Sciences
2101 Constitution Avenue, N.W., Washington, D.C. 20418 U.S.A.

Library of Congress Catalog Card Number 74-10125
International Standard Book Number 0-309-02242-8

Printed in the United States of America

Acknowledgments

The committee wishes to thank our cosponsoring institutions' staff members for their assistance with the many details that made it possible for each seminar to run smoothly. In particular, we wish to thank the following people:

In Colombo, Sri Lanka, for help with the South Asia Seminar from the Marga Institute, Mr. Chandra Soysa (Director), Mrs. Olga Ramasamy, Mr. A. C. Wijenathan, and Mr. M. M. Mohideen; and from the Colombo Plan Bureau, Brigadier General A. B. Connelly (then Director), Dr. John Edlefsen (then Regional Population Adviser), and Mrs. Malini Balasingham.

In Yugoslavia, Dr. Pavao Novosel of the Faculty of Political Science, University of Zagreb, made the seminar arrangements, and Miss Srebrenka Zuric assisted him during the Middle East Seminar in Dubrovnik.

In Jamaica, Mr. Hector Wynter (then Projects Director) and Mrs. E. J. Rafferty of the Association of Caribbean Universities and Research Institutes, and Mrs. Joyce Byles gave expert help with the Latin America–Commonwealth Caribbean Seminar in Montego Bay.

In Nairobi, Kenya, Dr. J. Mugo Gachuhi (then Acting Director) and Mr. Joshua Randiki of the Institute for Development Studies, University of Nairobi, and Mrs. Wambui Kinuthia carried out the arrangements for the Africa Seminar.

Dr. Roland Force (Chairman, Executive Committee, Pacific Science Council) and his assistant Brenda Bishop, both of the Pacific Science Association, and also Dr. Mercedes Concepcion, Dean of the Population Institute, University of the Philippines, and President of the Organization of Demographic Associates, cooperated in making arrangements for the Southeast Asia Seminar in Manila, Philippines.

For the conference interpretation services we wish to thank Mrs. Nicole Dizdarevic and Mrs. Gabrijela Vidan (French/English) in Dubrovnik; Miss Lidia Valdivia-Mendoza, Mrs. Isabel de Rivas, and Mr. Bosco Nedelcovic (Spanish/English) in Montego Bay, Jamaica; and Madame Jo Chevassus and Miss Sanda Iliescu (French/English) in Nairobi. Mr. Nedelcovic also translated some seminar documents (Spanish/English).

Mr. Thomas Lyons, formerly with the Office of Population, U.S. Agency for International Development (AID), Washington (now with the AID Mission in Lagos, Nigeria), and Dr. Steven Sinding of the same office generously gave their time and cooperated fully with the staff.

We are particularly indebted to Mrs. Pushpa Nand Schwartz, the Project Coordinator, for her sustained dedication and skill in supervising the myriad aspects of seminar organization and logistics, as well as report preparation.

Marlene Staley was responsible for the many painstaking details in preparing and typing the report. Jane Lecht edited the manuscript.

Many other individuals offered useful suggestions and guidance at various stages of this project, and we warmly acknowledge their advice.

MYRON WEINER, *Chairman*
W. MURRAY TODD, *Project Director*

INTERNATIONAL STEERING COMMITTEE
FOR THE SEMINARS ON POPULATION POLICY

Members

MYRON WEINER, Professor of Political Science, Massachusetts Institute of Technology, Cambridge, Massachusetts, U.S.A., *Chairman*

NAZLI CHOUCRI, Associate Professor of Political Science, Massachusetts Institute of Technology, Cambridge, Massachusetts, U.S.A. (Citizen of the Arab Republic of Egypt)

PAUL DEMENY, Vice President, The Population Council, New York, New York, U.S.A. (former Director, East–West Population Institute, University of Hawaii)

ARMAND V. FABELLA, Chairman, Presidential Commission on Reorganization; Vice President, Jose Rizal College, Manila, Philippines

LUIS LEÑERO OTERO, Director, Instituto Méxicano de Estudios Sociales, México, D.F., México

BETTY P. MATHEWS, Professor of Health Education, University of Washington, Seattle, Washington, U.S.A.

W. PARKER MAULDIN, Vice President, The Population Council, New York, New York, U.S.A.

ASOK MITRA, Secretary to the President of India, New Delhi, India

PAVAO NOVOSEL, Professor of Political Science, University of Zagreb, Zagreb, Yugoslavia

CHUKUKA OKONJO, Professor of Economics, Dean, Faculty of the Social Sciences, University of Nigeria, Nsukka, East Central State, Nigeria

ROGER REVELLE, Director, Center for Population Studies, Cambridge, Massachusetts, U.S.A.; Member, Commission on International Relations, National Academy of Sciences–National Research Council; *ex officio* member, International Steering Committee

GEORGE STOLNITZ, Professor of Economics, Indiana University, Bloomington, Indiana, U.S.A.

Staff

PUSHPA NAND SCHWARTZ, *Project Coordinator*

W. MURRAY TODD, *Project Director*

Population Policy Seminars, 1973

Region	Cosponsors
SOUTH ASIA 12–16 February Colombo, Sri Lanka	Marga Institute; Colombo Plan Bureau Colombo, Sri Lanka
MIDDLE EAST 30 April–4 May Dubrovnik, Yugoslavia	Yugoslav Council of Academies of Sciences and Arts Zagreb, Yugoslavia
LATIN AMERICA–COMMONWEALTH CARIBBEAN 20–24 August Montego Bay, Jamaica	Association of Caribbean Universities and Research Institutes Kingston, Jamaica
AFRICA 10–14 September Nairobi, Kenya	Institute for Development Studies University of Nairobi Nairobi, Kenya
SOUTHEAST ASIA 27 November–1 December Manila, Philippines	Organization of Demographic Associates Manila, Philippines; Pacific Science Association Honolulu, Hawaii, U.S.A.

Contents

I   INTRODUCTION   1

II SOUTH ASIA SEMINAR ON POPULATION POLICY   7
      Major Themes, 9
      Urbanization and Housing, 13
      Employment, 15
      Education, Health, and Welfare, 17
      Making Policy Work, 19
      Participants, 22

III MIDDLE EAST SEMINAR ON POPULATION POLICY   24
      Perceptions of Population Problems, 24
      Making Policy Work, 25
      Leadership, Politics, and Administration, 29
      Population Education and Family Life, 30
      Status of Women, 31
      Education and Employment, 32
      Urban Growth, 34
      Islam: Inconsistencies and Reinterpretations, 35
      Foreign Aid, 37
      Participants, 38

IV LATIN AMERICA–COMMONWEALTH CARIBBEAN SEMINAR
    ON POPULATION POLICY   40
        Perceptions of Population Problems, 41
        Spectrum of Development Policies, 44
        Population-Related Policies, 45
        Women and the Family, 46
        Role of the Catholic Church, 48
        Foreign Aid, 48
        Policy Options, 49
        Participants, 53

V   AFRICAN SEMINAR ON POPULATION POLICY   55
        Major Themes, 57
        Perceptions of Population Problems, 58
        Population Policies in Some Nations, 61
        Status of Women, 65
        Foreign Aid, 66
        Making Policy Work, 67
        Policy Constraints, 69
        Participants, 71

VI SOUTHEAST ASIA SEMINAR ON POPULATION POLICY   73
        Perceptions of Population Problems, 73
        Sociocultural Aspects, 75
        Urbanization and Migration, 76
        Status of Women, 78
        Foreign Aid, 79
        Constituencies for Population Policy, 80
        Making Policy Work, 80
        Policy Options, 82
        Participants, 84

VII SUMMARY AND COMMITTEE REFLECTIONS   86
        What Is Population Policy?, 86
        How Some Developing Countries View Population
            Growth, 87
        Population Policies, 91
        Policy Formulation and Administration: Actors and
            Constituencies, 101
        Religious Constraints, 103
        Foreign Aid, 104
        Policy Directions for the Future, 105

Introduction

I

This is a report of what some people in developing countries think about population policy—a topic that is emerging as a subject of critical concern to governments of those countries.

Most countries have policies that affect population variables in some way, but there is little agreement among policymakers and scholars on exactly what these policies are and how they work. Although many countries have gained experience in designing programs to study and influence some population trends (e.g., demographic surveys, censuses, and fertility-limitation programs) and there is a vast body of literature concerning these matters, research and analysis on the policy aspects of population issues are inadequate. How are population policies made—both those designed to influence demographic variables and those that respond to population changes? Who makes them and in response to whose demands or perceived needs? How are they executed? What are the alternative policy options or long-term choices?

The project from which this report is derived was begun in mid-1972 in the Office of the Foreign Secretary of the U.S. National Academy of Sciences,* under a contract with the U.S. Agency for International De-

*The National Academy of Sciences–National Research Council (NAS–NRC) is a private institution chartered by the U.S. Congress in 1863 to advise the government on scientific and technical policy questions.

The Academy published an earlier study: *Rapid Population Growth: Consequences and Policy Implications:* Vol. 1, *Summary & Recommendations;* Vol. 2, *Research Papers.* Baltimore, Md., and London: Johns Hopkins Press (1971). 696 pp.

velopment. Its purpose was to create a forum in which the social and political analysts, scholars, and leaders of developing countries could express their opinions and experiences and share in the opinions and experiences of others. The members of the International Steering Committee who guided the project throughout are listed at the front of this report.

In 1973 five regional seminars were held in different parts of the developing world. The seminars did not provide complete coverage of any region. The project was neither a scientifically designed opinion poll nor was it an effort to report the views of population experts. In all, more than 100 individuals from 37 countries took part in the discussions.

Regional and research–academic institutions with interests similar to those of the NAS–NRC cosponsored each seminar. They helped to select participants and issue invitations, and they undertook the necessary planning and organizational work. Cosponsors, dates, and places for each seminar are listed in the front of this report.

The five seminars were small and informal so that a wide range of topics could be explored and each participant would have a chance to express his views. The seminars lasted 5 days. They were conducted in English in South Asia and Southeast Asia, English and French in the Middle East and Africa, and English and Spanish in the Latin America–Commonwealth Caribbean Seminar, with simultaneous interpretation for the last three.

Participants were selected from many disciplines and backgrounds. Among them were policymakers from government ministries of health, planning, education, manpower or labor, and rural development; there were social workers, lawyers, journalists, city planners, religious and civic leaders, medical doctors, nurses, and scholars from demography, economics, sociology, political science, and geography. The mix of disciplines, professions, and interests in each seminar is shown in Table 1.

The goal was to discuss population policy issues from many points of view. We sought the perspectives of those who make policy and are responsible for its administration, those who advise policymakers and conduct research, those who grapple with problems resulting from population change, those who report on or observe the effects of policy, and those who are affected by policy and should have more influence on its formulation.

The names of invitees were gathered from many sources: social science and population literature, professional societies and organizations, universities, international organizations, the cosponsoring institutions, and the personal knowledge of interested people.

Each seminar was limited to 20–25 participants selected from five to nine countries in a region to permit full individual participation. We tried, however, in each instance to have participants from countries with the largest population in the region and others from countries considered unique or special, either because of ethnic composition or innovative policies. On occasion one or more experts or observers were invited to attend a seminar.

With the invitation, each participant received a set of questions asking for a brief, informal memorandum (5–10 pages) in which they could either address all the questions or concentrate on those of special interest to the participant. The memoranda were circulated among the other participants and the steering committee for information only and are not being published. The following questions were asked:

1. *Population Problems*   Are there problems in your country resulting from changes in human fertility, mortality, or distribution of population?

2. *Population Policies or Responses and Their Effects*   What policies or programs (explicit or implicit) do you have in your country for dealing with these problems, and what are their underlying assumptions? What are the goals of these policies, and to what extent are these goals being met? Are these policies adequate? Are they working? Are these policies consistent with each other and with other national social and economic objectives? How is their effectiveness measured? Are you aware of any regional and international effects of the policies or programs pursued in your country and in others?

3. *Policy Administration: Actors and Constituent Groups*   How are population policies or programs created and implemented? What groups are affected by them? Who is making policy and in response to what, or to whose, needs? What are the economic, political, and cultural constraints affecting policy formulation and implementation? Are there some issues that should be included in population policy in your country but are not? What are they, and why are they not included?

4. *Policy Options*   What alternative or additional policy options or measures would you suggest? What would their benefits and costs be— economic, social, and political?

The questions and the requests for memoranda were devised to provide a common point of departure for discussion and to prepare the participants to examine population policy in a broad context. In addition, the memoranda gave participants specific information to help them understand the population situation in neighboring countries.

TABLE 1 Number of Participants in Population Policy Seminars by Region and Discipline, 1973

Region	Government Officials/ Policymakers				Social Scientists						Others			
	Agriculture	Education	Health, Social Welfare	Planning, Economics	Anthropology, Sociology, Geography	Demography	Economics	Education	Law	Political Science	City Planners	Journalists	Private Family Planning/Medical	Religious/ Civic Leaders
South Asia	1	1	2	2	2	3	4	1	1	1	1	1		
Middle East		1	2	1	3	2	4	1	1			3	4	
Caribbean and Latin America			2	1	1	3	3	3	1	1	2		2	2
Africa			3	4	3	2	1	2			3	1	1	1
Southeast Asia	1		2	1	2	3	3	2			2	1		1

Participants were also sent four or five published articles and chapters of books as background reading on population policy and descriptive material about the population issues in either one country in the region or the entire region. This, too, was to help provide a common starting point.

All seminars followed an agenda based on the four major questions. The seminar cochairmen (usually members of the steering committee and always one from the region) guided the discussion gently to ensure that the group explored information about each country's situation. Individuals with particular knowledge or working experience in a subject, such as city planning, the media, or rural development, were encouraged to explain unique problems or issues. This process expanded the participants' understanding of the implications and considerations involved in population policy.

At the end of each seminar, participants were asked to complete an evaluation questionnaire that included questions about the seminar method, organization, selection of participants, what they had learned from the seminar, and what improvements they would suggest. The responses provided many helpful suggestions. Most participants said that they had gained a broader understanding of population policy as a result of the seminar discussions. Initially, many were uneasy about being among people from different fields, but in the end they agreed that mixing the disciplines and professions helped them to look at problems in new ways.

After each seminar, the staff and seminar cochairmen prepared a draft report of the seminar discussions, with occasional factual information drawn from the memoranda. This draft was sent to each participant with a request for comments and suggestions for revision. The steering committee received the reports and incorporated the suggested revisions.

The seminar reports may not be completely consistent with facts or data on a country or region; they are meant to be a faithful summary of the actual discussions in the seminars. The themes and headings are not uniform from one seminar to the next because different issues are of greater or lesser importance in each region. Different emphases reveal regional differences.

Although few direct quotations are used in the seminar reports, all material in Chapters II–VI reflects the various views of seminar participants and not necessarily those of the steering committee.

The seminar reports are arranged in the order in which they were held in 1973. They are followed by the steering committee's summary and reflections.

The principal audience for this book is government policymakers and knowledgeable laymen. The activities and events leading to the 1974 United Nations' World Population Year and Conference—the myriad preparatory meetings, symposia, conferences, national and regional activities, both governmental and nongovernmental—have resulted in broad citizen interest and a desire for clear and readily understood information on population questions. We hope that the brief, impressionistic, and in some instances homely set of observations presented here will serve this interest.

As a committee, we tried to maintain, insofar as possible, a reportorial, objective view of the perceptions revealed by the participants in each seminar. We tried to refrain from offering "solutions," from injecting "facts" where we thought they were absent, and from making recommendations to the participants. We guaranteed the seminar participants anonymity for their remarks and assured them that we would not publish the memoranda they prepared for the seminar. Our goal is to report faithfully what 100 quite different people see, think, and say.

We believe that this effort to undertake a global experiment to learn how people in the developing world feel about population issues merited our time and effort and that of the participants and the co-sponsoring institutions. We hope the readers of this report will agree.

South Asia Seminar on Population Policy

II

Colombo, Sri Lanka, 12–16 February 1973
Marga Institute (Sri Lanka)
Colombo Plan Bureau (Sri Lanka)
National Academy of Sciences–National Research Council (U.S.A.)

The South Asia seminar, with participants from Bangladesh, India, Nepal, Pakistan, and Sri Lanka, took place in the midst of a succession of political and economic crises. Bangladesh had emerged, only a year earlier, as the newest country in the region, burdened with the human costs of a devastating war, dependence on other countries for famine relief and development assistance, and a harassed political leadership. A truncated Pakistan was recovering from war with India, a change in government, and a new set of internal political problems. India, too, was suffering from the enormous costs of the war, a substantial reduction in foreign assistance from the West, and a low economic growth rate. Sri Lanka, only 2 years earlier, had been troubled by a youth insurrection that not only strained her resources but inflicted a traumatic psychological impact on her left-of-center leadership. Moreover, the entire region, including portions of Nepal, Bangladesh, northern and western India, and Pakistan, had been affected by a succession of floods and droughts, crop failures, and an accompanying stagnation of industrial growth.

All participants agreed that current population growth rates in their countries are too high and expressed the need to reduce these rates of growth. Some emphasized the effects of population growth on efforts to increase the amount of food available to each person. Others emphasized the rise in unemployment as the generations born in the 1950s

TABLE 2 Five South Asian Countries: Recent Population Data

Country	Estimated Population, Mid-1960 (millions)	Estimated Population, 1-1-73 (millions)	Births per 1,000 Population, 1972	Deaths per 1,000 Population, 1972	Annual Natural Increase, 1972 (%)	Years To Double Population	Population under Age 15 (%)	Life Expectancy at Birth, 1972 (years)	Urban Population (%) 1970	Urban Population (%) 1985 Projected	Inhabitants per km², 1971	GNP per Capita at 1971 Market Prices (U.S. $)	Literate Population[a] (%)	Population per Physician (thousands)
Bangladesh	na[c]	76.43	45-50	18	2.7	26	>45	53	5	na	510	70	22	5 (1972)
India	429.02	576	37	15	2.2	32	42	51	20	25	168	110	34	6 (1971)
Nepal	9.25	11.96	45	22	2.3	30	42	43	5	7	80	90	9	49 (1970)
Pakistan	100.17[b]	64.46	45	16	2.9	24	>45	54	23	na	82	130	16	4 (1969)
Sri Lanka	9.89	13.06	30	8	2.2	32	40	65	20	25	193	100	82	3.9 (1971)

[a]Various years, 1965-1973.

[b]Figures include West Pakistan and East Pakistan (Bangladesh).

[c]na = not available.

SOURCES: Data assembled from the following:

International Bank for Reconstruction and Development. *World Bank Atlas.* Washington, D.C., 1973.

Nortman, Dorothy. *Population and Family Planning Programs: A Factbook.* Reports on Population/Family Planning, Number Two (Fifth Edition). The Population Council, New York, September 1973.

U.N. Department of Economic and Social Affairs, Statistical Office. *Demographic Yearbook 1972.* New York, 1973.

U.N. Department of Economic and Social Affairs, Statistical Office. *Statistical Yearbook 1972.* New York, 1973.

U.N. Educational, Scientific and Cultural Organization. *Statistical Yearbook 1972.* Paris, 1973.

U.S. Agency for International Development. *Population Program Assistance.* Bureau for Population and Humanitarian Assistance, Office of Population, Washington, D.C., December 1972.

U.S. Bureau of the Census, International Statistical Programs Center. *Recent Demographic Estimates for the Countries and Regions of the World.* Research Document No. 6. U.S. Department of Commerce, Social and Economic Statistics Administration, Washington, D.C., Preliminary Draft, January 1974.

enter the labor market; still others, the effects of population growth on the expansion of towns and cities in South Asia. Discussion centered on what steps can be taken, how efforts to influence rates of population growth are related to development policy, what can be done to cope with some of the effects of population growth, whether and how population movements to urban areas also constitute a problem, and what, if any, government interventions will make a difference.

Table 2 summarizes population data on the region.

MAJOR THEMES

The seminar identified eight critical policy concerns in South Asia.

1. *Constituencies*   There are no significant political constituencies for family planning in South Asia. Thus, aside from the bureaucracies engaged in administering family-planning programs, the impetus and the sustaining vigor of these programs comes from the active efforts of a small, well-educated, and influential group among those who hold political power and, for several South Asian countries, from foreign influences, particularly the World Bank, U.S. foundations, and bilateral aid programs. Neither family-planning programs nor population policies find a place in the election platforms of political parties, nor are the issues much discussed in political forums.

A tip of this political iceberg became visible in Bangladesh: After separation from Pakistan, it was politically unwise for a while to promote family planning, which had been "imposed" by the previous government.

The underlying reality, however, lies in the values and interests of the people of the region. Apparently, the vast majority do not put fertility limitation very high on their scale of present needs and wants. Though many people know what fertility limitation is, only a very few are convinced that it would benefit them and their families. The "value" of an extra child still seems to outweigh the "cost" of the child.

2. *Status of Women*   The health, education, and employment of women and, most fundamentally, the emancipation of women from traditional roles were regarded as keys to both remaking the societies in this region and reducing fertility. On this, the group—mainly men— agreed, and gave the sensitive topic considerable attention. But the policymaker's dilemma—how to find jobs for women in the midst of a vast army of unemployed and underemployed ablebodied men—could

not be resolved. There are times when the goals of social justice seem to run head on into the objectives of development planning, and perhaps this is one of them. Considerable thought was brought to bear on how women might work, but not in competition with men. Teaching in elementary schools in Bangladesh was one suggestion; placing one female teacher in each of the country's 30,000 schools would have a remarkable effect on both education and the role of women.

There was some agreement that attempts to delay the age of marriage, either through law or persuasion, would be futile as long as most young girls are neither in school nor gainfully employed. If the Chinese have succeeded in delaying the age of marriage, it is probably because they are providing alternatives for their young women. In other words, the participants saw the question of influencing the age of marriage as linked with the larger question of employment policies.

3. *Urbanization*   Regarded as a bane by most participants, urban migration was seen as the natural result of a rural labor force that grows faster than rural employment. The seminar had difficulty identifying population policies that come to grips with rapid urban growth as a major social force, but participants mentioned several urban development schemes that may be worth trying experimentally. At least one, described later, is self-financing and self-sustaining. However, because agriculture is the economic base of the region, the rural situation is enormously important and will continue to pervade all planning and projecting. Rural development is most difficult in areas where the physical infrastructure, such as roads and irrigation, is least developed.

4. *Incentive Schemes*   Although this seminar did not dwell long on analyzing current or proposed family-planning programs, an intense interest emerged in incentive schemes to reward people for reducing fertility. The most attractive idea was paying a woman a small sum every month she is not pregnant. A No-Birth Bonus Scheme is being tried in Coonoor, in the Nilgiris Hills area of Tamilnadu, India, among women on tea estates. It is too early to assess its effectiveness, but it looks promising and is also proving a desirable device for achieving more equitable income distribution. Moreover, the participants said that such incentive schemes might help to develop a political constituency for family planning because of the apparent interest of many politicians in achieving greater equality of income. The enormous costs of transfer payments of this sort instilled doubt in some economists, but all agreed that finding ways to stimulate interest and achieve sustained results in fertility limitation were of the highest priority.

5. *Old-Age Security*   Coupled with the interest in incentives for fertility limitation was acceptance in principle of social security, or

state-provided old-age pension schemes, as a way to reduce the traditional need for sons in one's old age. At the same time, it was recognized that universal social security will be beyond the capacity of South Asian countries for a long time. In the cultures of South Asia the family is still the basic social unit, and the traditional roles of parents, children, close relatives, and the multigeneration household preclude relegating the aged and infirm to nonfamilial surroundings. But the measure of independence that social security and pensions confer does not inevitably mean separating the old from the household; such measures may even strengthen traditional relationships with the new bond of self-respect. However, the costs of social security schemes were seen as prohibitive and, by some, as socially undesirable. As one participant said, "An old man eats no more than a baby." The "cost" of superannuation or old age is not sharply perceived and is often disguised by the "value" imputed to old members of a family who are beyond the productive labor force age but honored for their familial guidance and authority.

6. *Approach to Development*   Population policy is an integral part of development policies and programs. A developmental approach that would bring reduced birth rates is needed, in contrast to a solely fertility-limiting approach, which the participants saw as negative and narrow.

From the point of view of politics and national goals, there was consensus that family-planning programs in isolation would be rejected, especially if offered from the outside. Only within a program in which fertility limitation is coupled with improved nutrition, maternal and child health, enhancement of the status of women, education, and, above all, employment, will family planning have any impact on the present or future of the region.

7. *Employment*   Population policy parallels development policy in giving primary attention to the question of providing jobs. The possibility of public works programs to build the infrastructure of desperately poor rural areas was discussed at some length, as were some other labor-intensive schemes. A whole range of public policies affecting investment, imports, and education should be combined in a vigorous attack on the unemployment problem. The growing numbers of educated unemployed are also a disturbing element of the situation. Beyond a number of particular special solutions offered, the participants were not optimistic about finding satisfactory ways to cope with both rural and urban unemployment and underemployment; the magnitude of the employment problem, it was recognized, will most likely increase in the immediate future.

The seminar codified the following as the corollaries of rapid population growth and their consequences.

Corollaries	Consequences
Increasing number of people	Environmental problems Need to increase food production
Larger family size	Malnutrition of children High cost of education and services
Larger proportion of children	High dependency Lower per capita income
Increasing number of families	Decrease in size of farms Increase in landless labor Poor income distribution
Increasing density in rural areas	Unemployment Agricultural deterioration Conflicts in land use
Rapid increase in numbers seeking employment	Large investments to create jobs
Differentials of fertility in ethnic groups	Political instability, ethnic conflicts

8. *Remodeling Society*   The ultimate policy question is, how can the people of South Asia create the sort of society that could act effectively on these problems? Paralleling the search for the necessary components of social and economic development is a doubt that current political forms and philosophies can cope with the problems. A few asked bluntly whether, in light of the desperate poverty that exists, the costs of democracy and of laissez-faire policies are too high.

The influence of what is known of social progress in the People's Republic of China is apparently enormous. The example of a vigorous and self-confident China, moving onto the world stage after over 20 years of isolation, has altered perceptions of how to get things done. Self-reliance, discipline, and patriotism are ideas with a new and powerful magnetism. Fully aware of the denial of individual choice in the

Chinese system and with no illusions about the differences in cultural traditions between South Asia and China, the participants were nevertheless deeply conscious of the need for powerful motivations to change their societies.

Clearly, a period of profound questioning of old values is at hand, and political and social leaders must demonstrate commitment, example, and imagination to guide their societies toward "social justice."

URBANIZATION AND HOUSING

The need for spatial policies and spatial planning with sectoral planning is summed up in the question, where will the next half-billion-plus South Asians live by the end of the century? Opinions differed on what rates of urbanization are likely to occur in each country of the region, how much urbanization is desirable, how dispersed the pattern of urbanization should be, and what instruments are available to governments for influencing the rate and pattern of urbanization.

Two issues dominated the discussion: (1) What are the advantages and disadvantages of more urban growth, compared with further development of rural and semiurban areas? (2) What kinds of housing and other facilities can be provided in urban areas? Several policy elements are associated with these issues: costs, management, motivation, optimum scales of urban units, the relationship between provincial or district administration and urban centers, and feasibility of governing units' doing more than simply responding to massive needs for housing.

The point was made that most urban planning is based on a vision of society that looks like the top pyramid in Figure 1; whereas, in reality, it looks like the bottom pyramid. There is almost no low-cost housing for the masses existing at bare subsistence levels.

It is estimated that the urban population of India will double by 1985. A combination of land-use planning, city design, and individual construction in low-rise, high-density, linear settlements linked by public transportation to the labor market was advocated as one approach to urban development. This formula requires a minimum of public capital investment because it relies on individual investment and labor in constructing inexpensive individual dwellings made of easily obtainable local materials; the scheme is flexible because these units can be renewed periodically or expanded modestly when the need arises. Design, planning, and transportation are contrived to enhance the mobility of labor, locate public and private enterprises in optimum relation to each other, and create a self-financing flow of capital as the value of land appreciates. To some observers, the sheer size of the problem of providing homes for millions in places like Bombay and Karachi dictates the solution: building new towns or cities.

An alternative to large-scale urban development was advocated for Bangladesh, where there is little urbanization outside of Dacca and Chittagong. Small townships with local service industries and government establishments could be encouraged, all within walking distance of rural habitations. The goal of such "miniurbanization" would be to keep most of the town labor living on rural plots and to forestall mass migration into a few large, mushrooming cities.

Sri Lanka has a density problem, but its population has not migrated to the few cities in any substantial numbers. The current plan, in line with its largely agriculture-based economy, is to accentuate the impor-

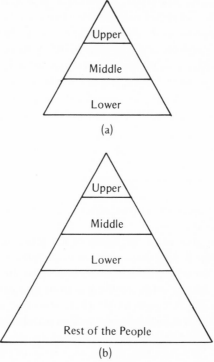

FIGURE 1   Income pyramids in (a) developed and (b) developing countries. Pyramid (a) assumes all people have regular incomes; in (b) the bottom layer has no regular income.

tance of small semirural, semiurban centers, as an alternative to intense urbanization in Colombo.

One participant spoke of various efforts in India to eliminate urban squatter settlements with a density over 1,000 per acre and to achieve a density of 200–300 per acre in the newer cities, especially in the new urban settlements outside Bombay. Space requirements for housing in South Asia may be less than in some other regions of the world because people are willing to live in accommodations with less than 30 square feet per person.

Some countries, particularly in Eastern Europe and more recently in Singapore, use housing availability as a disincentive to fertility and, in some countries, as an obstacle to marriage. This policy is not particularly applicable to the countries of South Asia, where local building materials are cheap and plentiful and the climate puts a minimum demand on the skills of the builder and investment by the occupant.

Most participants emphasized that, in light of existing conditions in urban employment and housing, further migration into large urban areas should be discouraged by dispersing industries into rural areas and small towns and by dispersing educational institutions. One or two participants remained unconvinced that urban growth was undesirable, arguing that urbanization was an important aspect of modernization and development. Moreover, the process of industrial and educational dispersal resulted in more, not less, urbanization, albeit in a more dispersed pattern.

EMPLOYMENT

One of the most visible and intractable policy problems for planners, legislators, and political leaders is employment. The seminar granted itself the freedom of a fuzzy definition of the term, agreeing only that employment in South Asia does not mean 220 8-hour days of work per year in the tradition of industrialized societies and that employment in agriculture varies greatly with cropping seasons and patterns. Underemployment was also left undefined. There was general recognition that nutritional and health deficiencies, as well as simple inefficiency, contribute to a picture of labor productivity that differs among the countries of the region and from the norms and standards of developed countries.

South Asian planners have thought of employment as an automatic side effect of economic development; now, with high rates of unemployment and large numbers entering the labor force, employment must be regarded as the central objective of planning. This point of view, held by participants from the three major countries of the region, led to a general agreement that employment rather than growth of national income must become the measure of development.

Statistical evidence presented at the seminar included the following: Employment in India is growing at the rate of 1.8–2.0 percent per year while the labor force grows about 2.5 percent per year. The labor:capital ratio–the demand for labor created per rupee invested–has been declining at the rate of 5 percent per year because of mechanization in industry and agriculture. Bengalis and Pakistanis in the seminar agreed that a similar general situation prevails in their countries.

Throughout the region the key question is, how can the rural sector absorb more of the existing and continually expanding labor force? The consensus of the seminar was that public works might provide a partial answer. India has made a substantial commitment to this policy in its present 5-year plan, which provides for the construction of roads, rural electrification, and wells for irrigation (and drinking water), that is, projects that generate employment and are productive. Otherwise, public works programs can be highly inflationary if they simply put money in the hands of poor people without increasing production of goods or services. However, public works programs have had little impact on employment to date. In actual practice, the few funds that have been provided are underspent. At the district level no organization exists that can create such projects. Nor are the unemployed politically organized into unions to demand the establishment of public works projects.

One participant said that, although there has been much talk of "intermediate technologies" to increase employment in productive ways, few such technologies have actually been developed and used. Furthermore, little is known about the economics of different technologies and their varying effects on employment. Some technologies brought into rural areas have increased both agricultural production and employment; others have increased production and reduced employment.

There were expressions of concern about the low rate of investment in India and its impact on employment. According to one participant, a large amount of "black money" (private funds that could be, but are not, invested productively) is available, but the government is either reluctant or powerless to "seize" the money; nor has it permitted the money to be invested privately on terms attractive to the investor. The results, due to a level of investment under 10 percent of gross national product (GNP) in recent years, are economic stagnation and an unemployment rate of 9 percent.

In Sri Lanka, the critical problem, aside from sheer numbers of unemployed and an unemployment rate of 12–13 percent, is unemployment of the educated. Curiously and tragically, the higher one's educational attainment in Sri Lanka, the greater the likelihood of being unemployed. The pertinent question is how to relate the curriculum and public investment in education to the manpower needs of the economy.

EDUCATION, HEALTH, AND WELFARE

One participant compared the wants of Indian villagers in 1954 with those in 1967. The results listed by priority follow:

1954	1967
1. School	1. Irrigation
2. Dispensary	2. Potable water
3. Potable water	3. Dispensary
4. Irrigation	4. School

Whether one concludes that in this 13-year span the villagers had acquired enough schools and dispensaries to mitigate their "felt needs" or that the results of education were such that they perceived their best interests to be improvement of land resources rather than human resources, there is some suggestion that social welfare does not loom as large in their aspirations today.

The seminar singled out the status, education, and health of women (including abortion); old-age pensions; and nutrition in its discussion of social and public welfare policies that might affect population variables.

Abortion was regarded as a desirable adjunct to any realistic attempt to reduce fertility because it is an extension of health services—not to be considered a population-control measure—and a part of the pattern of female emancipation. Inadequacy of facilities and trained personnel and the cultural setting, however, may preclude a massive abortion program in the Japanese or Hungarian mode. Raising the age of marriage to postpone childbearing was briefly discussed, as were the need for adequate sex education in the schools and the difficulty of applying these ideas in rural areas.

Education of women and general improvement in their status should be goals of policy and political action. Developing a political constituency in support of such action, even among women, however, was believed to be a long and arduous task, and the capacity of the current structures of society to absorb radical changes in women's status is questionable.

Maternal and child health, nutrition education, free and wide dissemination of contraceptive information and materials, and promotion of the small-family norm via the communication network of health service delivery were all cited as policy areas that are now not fully exploited. They need a great deal of streamlining and they also need to be decentralized to the district or even village level through local grass roots administrative devices. It would be interesting to know more about how the local administrative machinery in the Chinese system works.

In all the countries of South Asia the demand is great for both social welfare and economic growth. All participants were convinced that establishing a floor on income is politically acceptable throughout South Asia and that such a policy, if economically feasible, would be likely to reduce fertility rates. Provisions for health services, primary education, nutritional programs, and even food subsidies could reduce infant mortality and infant morbidity, and increase acceptance of small-family norms. Since such policies have actually been pursued by the government of Sri Lanka, considerable attention was given to examining the consequences of these policies on the well-being of low-income groups, fertility behavior, and economic growth. The major policy issue is, how does a country invest in social development in a way that contributes to, rather than undermines, economic growth? The Sri Lanka participants said that social welfare programs in their country had met with the following consequences:

1. Although it is difficult to prove, social welfare programs probably contributed to the declining fertility rate in Sri Lanka, which is the lowest in South Asia.

2. Heavy expenditures on social services reduced the resources available for investment that might have generated a higher economic growth rate.

3. The pattern of social welfare policies and expenditures in some instances, according to one participant, may actually have reduced the earnings of the poor. For example, government-provided consumption subsidies of rice for every citizen depressed the price of rice for farmers

in the open market and acted as a disincentive to more production. The import-substitution policy in consumer goods raised the prices to consumers. The large investment in education along with the low rate of economic growth increased the number of unemployed, especially educated unemployed who do not wish to work in agriculture.

4. Social welfare policies probably prevented a rise in land fragmentation, but they did not prevent a rise in unemployment. Educational policies merely transferred the population problem from land fragmentation and disguised unemployment in the countryside to open unemployment of the educated in urban areas. With an estimated literacy rate of about 80 percent, as much as 12–13 percent of Sri Lanka's labor force is now visibly unemployed.

A participant from Bangladesh suggested a minimum set of social welfare policies: establishing universal compulsory primary education; expanding health facilities; and reducing child labor. Each of these policies is socially desirable and consistent with a policy of encouraging fertility reduction. Another participant argued that these minimums were not sufficient; a far higher investment in social welfare is needed if there is to be a floor on incomes high enough to reduce fertility. Still another said that most government outlays in India are for irrigation and power, industry and agriculture, leaving less than 15 percent for health and education. Financial elbowroom is so tight that if more were spent on welfare schemes, investment in development would have to be cut—a policy of killing the goose that lays the golden eggs.

MAKING POLICY WORK

A famous Japanese economist, visiting with some top economists in India, was asked, "What is the key to Japan's economic success?" Expecting a complex economic analysis, the Indian economists were astonished to hear their Japanese guest reply, "There are two keys to our success: discipline and patriotism." To all the seminar participants the story was an apt description of the obstacles to effective policy formulation and execution in their countries.

The family planning policy process in one country of the region was described as follows: The Ministry of Health and Family Planning provides guidelines to the Directorate of Family Planning, which produces a plan. This plan is reviewed by the Planning Commission's family-planning section, which in turn may request outside evaluation. The key actors in the process are bureaucrats and technicians. There is little interest and virtually no participation on the part of the public or the local institutions. Policy is created in a vacuum of public apathy, overlaid with internal bureaucratic competition, and meddling by foreign experts. There are no public demands for family-planning services and no public awareness of the difficulties.

Other participants described population policy formulation in their countries in similar ways. Although the process differs from country to country as to the ministries and agencies involved, it suffers from the same ills everywhere.

There was consensus that no political party in the region could, for the present, make fertility reduction a central issue, and tacit agreement that the perceived political and cultural sensitivity of the topic made it an extremely difficult one for any party to espouse directly. The fertility-reduction targets that have been established and missed so regularly in South Asia are largely the creations of imaginative minds responding to donor-agency pressures to provide yardsticks.

In a discussion of urban-development policies, it was agreed that governments do not anticipate, but only respond to, problems. The governmental response is usually random because no clear analysis exists of what to do or why. Throughout the discussion of urban migration patterns and employment policy, it was manifest that knowledge about individual motivation is woefully inadequate. Yet, to learn either why people prefer one course to another or how to make certain actions more appealing than others, an understanding of individual motivation is crucial to the planning that underlies population policy.

A typical policy option that can affect population variables is compulsory education as a measure to reduce fertility by increasing the cost of children to parents through the reduction of child labor. Education, like other welfare objectives, however, should be promoted on the basis of its intrinsic merit and not just as a fertility-reduction technique. The question of making primary education universal, compulsory, and feasible was argued by those who believe it necessary to have the resources for the whole package (buildings, equipment, books, uniforms, meals, etc.) versus those who declared that with a banyan tree, a blackboard, and cheaply produced texts any village can set up a school.

This type of argument revealed a philosophical difference among the participants; in this context the Chinese model—which emphasizes self-reliance—again appeared to weigh most heavily. The argument led to the question of how South Asian societies can be transformed to cope with their problems.

One group in the seminar appeared to favor measures to increase the efficiency of current national development efforts, pinning hopes on public works to provide employment and on greatly enhanced communication to motivate individual families to reduce fertility as health and nutrition improve. The other group, emphasizing self-help and income equalization, insisted that a grass roots politicization of the villagers must happen first. Although centrally managed, public works must be structured and sustained through village, district, and other local community organizations that manage their collective lives.

Participants frequently spoke of their countries' lack of adequate organizational capabilities and of political constraints at work when any policies are devised. The problem of organizational capabilities arises not only in the usual framework of the administrative structure but also in the more fundamental matter of discipline and motivation. Whether they talked about saving and investment, effective public works programs, reorganizing the school curricula, increasing productivity in the factories, or changing the age of marriage through law or persuasion, participants seemed to feel that motivations are weak and that few national political leaders, even if politically secure, are in a position to impose a sense of discipline on their people.

Several participants spoke of the inherent weakness of democratic political systems for generating motivation and discipline, at least in South Asian countries. One participant said that democratic governments can provide social services, expand education, carry out policies to increase consumption, and establish an income floor, but they cannot readily undertake programs to cut back consumption in favor of investment, legislate new inheritance customs, limit the age of marriage and enforce the limit, encourage labor to be more productive, or improve the quality of the educational system.

Participants agreed that their governments' policies should be more responsive to some major adverse effects of rapid population growth: high unemployment, low levels of primary school enrollment, inadequate rural health facilities, and a worsening of income distribution. Such policies are politically acceptable to the extent that they contribute to a more equitable distribution of the benefits of development. Moreover, they are likely to have the effect of reducing fertility, mortality, and rural migration to urban areas—all socially and economically desirable objectives. The policymaker's task then is to make population-responsive policies into population-influencing policies.*

*For a definition of population-responsive and population-influencing policies, see pages 86–87.

PARTICIPANTS

MR. K. D. ARIYADASA, Deputy Director General of Education, Curriculum Development Centre, Ministry of Education, Government of Sri Lanka, Colombo, Sri Lanka

DR. KHEM BAHADUR BISTA, Senior Officer, Centre for Economic Development and Administration, Kathmandu, Nepal

DR. SWADESH BOSE, Acting Director, Bangladesh Institute of Development Economics, Dacca, Bangladesh

MRS. SUMA CHITNIS, Reader and Head, Department of Research in Sociology, Tata Institute of Social Sciences, Bombay, India

MR. CHARLES CORREA, Indian Institute of Architects, Bombay, India

DR. GODFREY GUNATILLEKE, Vice Chairman, Board of Governors and Director, Marga Institute, Colombo, Sri Lanka

DR. SULTAN S. HASHMI, Chief, General Demography Section, Population Division, Economic Commission for Asia and the Far East, United Nations, Bangkok, Thailand (Citizen of Pakistan)

DR. S. Y. S. B. HERAT, Assistant Director, Maternal and Child Health, Government of Sri Lanka, Colombo, Sri Lanka

DR. ROUNAQ JAHAN, Department of Political Science, University of Dacca, Dacca, Bangladesh

DR. M. S. JILLANI, Regional Adviser on Social Development Planning, Economic Commission for Asia and the Far East, United Nations, Bangkok, Thailand (Citizen of Pakistan)

MR. A. Z. OBAIDULLAH KHAN, Secretary, Ministry of Rural Development and Cooperation, Government of Bangladesh, Dacca, Bangladesh

PROFESSOR RAJ KRISHNA, Department of Economics, University of Rajasthan, Jaipur, India

DR. ASOK MITRA, Secretary to the President of India, Rashtrapati Bhavan, New Delhi, India

MRS. SIVA OBEYSEKERA, Deputy Minister, Ministry of Health, Government of Sri Lanka, Colombo, Sri Lanka

DR. ZUBEIDA ZAFAR OMER, Education and Research Department, University of the Punjab, Lahore, Pakistan

MR. HAROUN ER RASHID, Consultant, International Bank for Reconstruction and Development, Bangkok, Thailand (Citizen of Bangladesh)

MR. S. SELVARATNAM, Adviser, Sociology, Ministry of Planning, Government of Sri Lanka, Colombo, Sri Lanka

MR. B. GEORGE VERGHESE, Editor-in-Chief, *The Hindustan Times*, New Delhi, India

DR. PRAVIN M. VISARIA, Department of Economics, University of Bombay, Bombay, India

OBSERVERS

MRS. MALINI BALASINGHAM, Assistant to Regional Population Adviser, Colombo Plan Bureau, Colombo, Sri Lanka

MR. R. K. SRIVASTAVA, Senior ILO Adviser on Manpower and Employment to the Ministry of Planning, Government of Sri Lanka, Colombo, Sri Lanka

DR. MAGNUS STIERNBORG, Adviser, Family Planning, Swedish International Development Authority, Stockholm, Sweden

MR. E. L. WIJEMANNE, Director of Education (Planning), Ministry of Education, Government of Sri Lanka, Colombo, Sri Lanka

REPRESENTATIVES OF COSPONSORING ORGANIZATIONS

BRIG. GEN. A. B. CONNELLY, Director, Colombo Plan Bureau, Colombo, Sri Lanka

DR. JOHN EDLEFSEN, Regional Population Adviser, Colombo Plan Bureau, Colombo, Sri Lanka

DR. ROGER REVELLE, Director, Center for Population Studies, Harvard University, Cambridge, Massachusetts, U.S.A.; *ex officio* Member, NAS-NRC International Steering Committee; *Seminar Cochairman*

MRS. PUSHPA NAND SCHWARTZ, NAS-NRC, Washington, D.C., U.S.A.; *Project Coordinator*

MR. CHANDRA SOYSA, Director, Marga Institute, Colombo, Sri Lanka; *Seminar Coordinator*

MR. W. MURRAY TODD, NAS-NRC, Washington, D.C., U.S.A.; *Project Director*

DR. MYRON WEINER, Department of Political Science, Massachusetts Institute of Technology, Cambridge, Massachusetts, U.S.A.; Chairman, NAS-NRC International Steering Committee; *Seminar Cochairman*

Middle East Seminar on Population Policy

III

Dubrovnik, Yugoslavia, 30 April–4 May 1973
Yugoslav Council of Academies of Sciences and Arts
National Academy of Sciences–National Research Council (U.S.A.)

Although the people of the Middle East have many common bonds, particularly in their dominant religion, Islam, there are marked differences in population characteristics and government responses. Population size and available resources vary greatly among these countries. Generally, the oil-producing countries have the smallest populations, and countries with the least resources have the biggest populations. Population size ranges from 930,000 in Kuwait to about 35,000,000 in Egypt (Table 3).

Seminar participants came from Afghanistan, Arab Republic of Egypt, Iran, Jordan, Kuwait, Lebanon, Tunisia, Turkey, and Yugoslavia. Although Yugoslavia is not part of the Middle East, it was included in this seminar because it was the seminar venue. Moreover, it has a sizable Moslem minority, as well as other ethnic groups.

PERCEPTIONS OF POPULATION PROBLEMS

Seminar participants saw the present high population growth rates as a problem in all their countries, except for Kuwait and Yugoslavia. Yugoslavia has a relatively low overall growth rate; Kuwait feels a need for more people, particularly more skilled labor. In the other countries present population growth rates and increasing migration to cities will

24

aggravate problems in the future, jeopardizing planned economic and social objectives by creating large dependent populations who press on scarce resources for "demographic investments," such as education, health, and housing.

Annual population growth rates in the Moslem countries range from about 2 to 4 percent, except in Kuwait, which has averaged an increase of more than 10 percent for more than 10 years because of its huge inmigration. Mortality rates will probably decline fairly quickly in several countries, and even higher rates of population growth will result.

Outside the oil-rich nations, population pressure on resources is keenly felt. Jordan imports two thirds of its food requirements, and its resource-poor economy has to cope with 50,000 new jobseekers a year. About 30 percent of its population is enrolled in school. The dependency burden is high; one person supports five. Egypt and Turkey have revised their planned economic growth targets because in each plan period rapid population growth contributed to shortfalls. Other countries, such as Iran and Tunisia, explicitly take population growth and distribution into account in their development planning and have adopted fertility-limiting policies and programs to lessen rates of population growth.

In most countries continuing migration to cities is overloading public services and increasing unemployment. Serious problems have resulted from two massive forced refugee movements to Jordan in 1948 and 1967, particularly to the cities; the impact of this migration is intensified by high rates of natural increase in all groups. Jordan's population has doubled in 20 years. Throughout the Middle East urban growth rates have been high, from 4 to 10 percent a year, with an exceptional 18 percent in Kuwait City.

The notion that economic development will eventually lead to a decline in population growth was emphatically answered. The countries of this region cannot wait for economic development. Long before a modern, industrialized economy is achieved, population growth will jeopardize economic and social stability.

MAKING POLICY WORK

Formulating policy and then carrying it out is a long, slow process, hence the importance of starting now and looking beyond present constraints to learn what policies will be needed in a few years. This need places great demands on governments burdened with pressing,

TABLE 3 Nine Middle East Countries: Recent Population Data

Country	Estimated Population, Mid-1960 (millions)	Estimated Population, 1-1-73 (millions)	Births per 1,000 Population, 1972	Deaths per 1,000 Population, 1972	Annual Natural Increase, 1972 (%)	Years To Double Population	Population under Age 15 (%)	Life Expectancy at Birth, 1972 (years)	Urban Population (%) 1970	Urban Population (%) 1985 Projected	Inhabitants per km², 1971	GNP per Capita at 1971 Market Prices (U.S. $)	Literate Population[a] (%)	Population per Physician (thousands)
Afghanistan	13.80	18.08	51	27	2.4	29	44	40	7	9	27	80	8	18.7 (1971)
Egypt	25.92	34.71	35	13	2.2	32	42	53	43	51	34	220	26	2.0 (1971)
Iran	21.52	32.78	48	16	3.2	22	45	53	41	52[b]	18	450	34	3.3 (1973)
Jordan	1.70	2.47	46	13	3.3	21	46	55	48	na[b]	24	260	32	3.8 (1970)
Kuwait	0.28	0.93	43	7	3.6	19	43	67	80	na	52	3,860	55	1.1 (1971)
Lebanon	2.11	3.01	40	9	3.1	22	43	61	60	na	276	660	86	1.5 (1969)
Tunisia	3.89	5.42	38	13	2.5	28	45	55	43	52	31	320	30	5.5 (1971)
Turkey	27.51	37.74	39	13	2.6	27	42	57	37	45	46	340	51	2.0 (1971)
Yugoslavia	18.40	20.84	18	9	1.0	73	27	67	37	53	81	730	80	0.9 (1971)

[a]Various years, 1965–1973.
[b]na = not available.
SOURCES: See Table 2, p. 8.

immediate problems and administrative constraints, some of which are noted later. The consensus was that population policy should be viewed as a tool for social and economic welfare, not as an end in itself.

Bureaucratic problems often hinder policy. In several countries the tradition of a trained, apolitical civil service is weak. Public records and statistics are seldom well kept. Research is not often sufficiently used in policy formulation. Too frequently, the bureaucracy provides answers the politicians wish to hear instead of information required for making sound policies.

In Tunisia and Egypt, each of which has a monolithic party structure, it has been possible to gain party endorsement and fieldwork by party personnel for family planning. In other countries specific policies sometimes are initiated because politicians seek short-term political gains or go along with a popular movement. Population programs, which seldom result in obvious political benefits or immediate results, often do not have strong political support.

Considerable attention was also given to nongovernmental channels and organizations. One participant said that informal networks, communal and parochial voluntary organizations should be recruited for population programs. Too often the people who implement policy ignore or even seek to alter or destroy these traditional institutions, which have been found to adapt to and absorb change remarkably well. Traditional neighborhoods and extended family networks that fulfill the need of rural migrants to belong to a community were described to illustrate how these institutions could complement public programs.

A study undertaken by a Yugoslavian participant pointed to the need to educate the policymaking elite on population issues. This elite views population less as a cause of economic and social problems than as a consequence. To achieve appropriate, integrated policies, policymakers must understand better the causal relationships between population and social and economic processes.

In regard to implementing population policy, the participants felt that an integrated approach to population issues should also consider population variables other than growth rates (e.g., changes in distribution and composition of population) in national economic and social planning. Some planning organizations, they noted, are unable to do this, partly because demographic data are inadequate or unreliable.

In an integrated approach various elements of policy are reasonably consistent and mutually reinforcing. Policies are usually administered by separate agencies, administrative units, or ministries. Typically, no overall or systematic review takes place to determine their impact on population. Several participants said, for example, that in their countries family-planning services, including abortion, were not integrated with maternal and child health or family health programs.

While there was consensus for an integrated approach to population issues, some participants pointed out that often family planning is given low priority when it is bureaucratically integrated in another program and not assigned a separate budget, or not given an important standing of its own as an identifiable program. There was some sentiment for separately funded, clearly identified population programs, with the responsibility for administering the program definitely assigned. Even so, many agencies should be involved, and the program should not be restricted to the ministry of health, as is often the case.

Integration of family planning with other policies, such as education and housing, was strongly endorsed in the belief that improving people's living conditions will motivate them to limit family size. For example, compulsory education, which removes children from the pool of family labor, has apparently lowered fertility in Jordan. Similarly, other measures such as family allowances, maternity benefits, and social security should be examined for their effects on fertility.

As a dramatic example of the need to integrate family planning with other programs, a participant told of a poor woman who came for help to a health center in Iran. When asked why she did not use contraceptives, she replied, "First, get my husband a job, then get my child into school, and then get my daughter married." Experience in Iran has been that mothers accept family-planning methods much more readily if they come into contact with them through a child welfare program— a nursery school, a child care center, or the community welfare center.

Tunisia has made a determined and systematic effort to coordinate such population-influencing policies: Family allowances are limited to four children. Social security is available to all persons. The age of marriage has been raised by increasing opportunities for women in education and employment. Iran and, to a lesser extent, Egypt and Turkey are making similar efforts; however, they are hindered by difficulties in administering programs and carrying them out, especially in remote areas.

Official family-planning programs and services to reduce fertility exist in Egypt, Iran, Tunisia, and Turkey. Little or no organized opposition to family planning programs is apparent in any of these countries. They are supported there and in most other countries in principle for reasons of health and human rights.

LEADERSHIP, POLITICS, AND ADMINISTRATION

The seminar emphasized the important role of a strong leader in initiating change and modernization. In Turkey and Egypt, strong national leaders, Ataturk and Nasser, led their countries through major and wide-ranging social changes. In Tunisia and Iran, measures in the last decade to bring about change in the status of women and in other population-related matters were strongly supported by popular national figures. President Bourguiba of Tunisia and the Shah of Iran, recognizing the impact of population on economic and social progress, became convinced of the need to reduce population growth rates. Their interest generated momentum in favor of family-planning programs. Social reforms and changes synchronized with, or responding to, family planning were possible because of vigorous advocacy by national leaders, as well as several influential private groups.

In Egypt the 1962 Charter formally recognized population as a major problem. No national measures were adopted, however, until 1965, when President Nasser, approached by a small group of citizens with detailed studies, became convinced of the need to act on population issues. The Supreme Council for Family Planning was established shortly thereafter, headed by the Prime Minister. One participant said, however, that family-planning efforts are not carried out with the vigor and tempo required to make them a success because of administrative inefficiency; lack of follow-up, evaluation, and coordination; and the preoccupation of the leadership with more pressing political problems. President Sadat has adopted family planning as an important aspect of national development and has urged the Arab Socialist Union Party to view family planning and literacy as community crusades. Literacy efforts have evoked great public enthusiasm; family planning, little.

Some national leaders recognize the importance of the population issue, but for political, administrative, and other reasons often find it difficult to move toward policy planning. For example, King Hussein of Jordan was one of 30 world leaders who signed the Statement on Population issued by the Secretary General of the United Nations in 1967, but there have been few policy developments in his country since. The refugee problem, administrative and bureaucratic constraints, and lack of information on demographic matters all account for the absence of policy. Any public discussion of reducing the population growth rate is highly sensitive in Jordan, where Palestinian refugees account for a sizable part of the population. Some politicians in Iran and Turkey, particularly at the height of the Cold War, believing that increasing population is directly related to national power, accentuated the political sensitivity of the population issue.

Recently in Jordan a National Population Commission was created, but what it does will depend on the information and advice it receives from several ministries. Officials in the ministries have the important task of educating policymakers to the need for a coherent population policy.

Different growth rates among various religious groups in Lebanon contribute to the sensitivity of the population issue. The delicate balance established among these groups makes even census-taking a highly political matter; the last official census was in 1932. The Lebanese government, it was said, does not involve itself in questions of family planning, and restrictive legislation still exists against the sale of contraceptives and abortion. Family planning is undertaken entirely by private groups and associations. Considerable unofficial contact takes place between the ranking officers in the key ministries and dedicated individuals in private associations concerned with population issues.

Some private associations, however, have been very active. In addition to the Lebanese example, the Afghan Women's Organization has been lobbying for family planning. Before official policy was formulated in Iran, a group of social workers and doctors engaged in community welfare work lobbied forcefully for a government-supported family-planning program and for legislation allowing abortion. Scholars and civil servants in Turkey helped to bring politicians around to face the need for policies to deal with rapid population growth. Unofficial concern and activity in population matters, though sometimes small, have been very important in motivating and channeling the development of public policy on population.

Nevertheless, the seminar agreed that a constituency for population policy—political or civic groups demanding or favoring family-planning programs or other measures related to population—is small or nonexistent in most countries of the Middle East.

POPULATION EDUCATION AND FAMILY LIFE

Overall, there is little education on population topics in the Middle East. The question of whether sex education is a desirable ingredient in literacy and public education programs was raised. To make such material more acceptable, it was suggested that sex education be incorporated in courses on family life and health. Because the vernacular of the Middle Eastern countries lacks appropriate terminology for sex education, an entirely new vocabulary must be developed if the subject is to be taught in schools.

Given the cultural sensitivities of these societies, this matter should be approached very carefully. Propagandizing about family planning, either through education or the news media, may disturb emotional attitudes and arouse opposition. Others think that it is possible to use the mass news media to introduce materials relating to family life and sex education. Indeed, materials relating to sex education, presented with considerable frankness, are regularly included in television broadcasts in Egypt and, apparently, are well received.

Songs, cartoons, plays, audiovisual materials, etc., were suggested as media to popularize the small-family norm. One participant pointed out that if the media create an increased demand for family planning and health services, facilities must be ready for the demand.

STATUS OF WOMEN

Most of the participants agreed on the desirability of improving the status of women and identifying policies to promote changes in attitudes toward women. With one or two exceptions, they saw the status of women as an issue of some priority for policy. The need to provide opportunities for female education and employment was frequently mentioned. It was noted that almost all countries are making some small attempts, those of Yugoslavia and Tunisia being the most extensive.

In the societies of the Middle East, as in most traditional societies, a male child is favored because of his greater potential as wage earner and contributor to his parents' security in old age. Status factors are also associated with this preference. Male offspring connote greater virility in the father; men who sire only females are viewed with slight disfavor.

Islamic divorce law, which discriminates against women, is a prime target for those seeking to improve the condition of women in Moslem countries. That many women fear divorce if they do not produce several children, especially boys, contributes to the pressures to bear children and reinforces tendencies toward large families.

Tunisia has extended the limit to which a Moslem nation has gone in revising traditional Islamic norms. Polygamy has been made illegal and abortion legalized. These changes were accomplished through legislative

measures, continuing public education to change attitudes, and attempts to create and promote female employment. A noticeable drop
in the Tunisian birth rate is attributed in part to the increased number
of working women who are highly motivated to limit family size, and
in part to the availability of abortion.

In Iran, too, polygamy has been made illegal, abortion recently
legalized, and efforts made to give women more opportunities for education and employment. But this situation is rare in the Middle East.
So deeply ingrained were traditional attitudes that efforts to improve
the condition of women in Afghanistan in the 1920s, according to one
participant, contributed to political turmoil and civil strife and for
some years continued to meet with great and organized resistance. In
many areas, perhaps, things have not changed much in the last 50
years.

Even in Lebanon, a modern country by many standards, female
participation in political life is limited. Only in 1955 was suffrage extended to include women who were not literate. A Lebanese woman
must still have the consent of a male head of the family to obtain a
passport for foreign travel. Participation of Lebanese women in the
labor force is high compared with other countries in the region: 23.8
percent for the 20- to 24-year-old age group, dropping progressively in
older ages and among the married from 15.3 percent for the 30–39
age group to 12.9 percent for 40–49 and to less than 10 percent for the
50–59 and 60–64 age groups. Regardless of educational level, women
do not participate in policy and decision making, nor are they encouraged to enter public life—a situation attributed to traditional attitudes and male opposition.

In discussing the problem of changing attitudes, one participant
made a strong case for increasing educational opportunities for females,
citing the significantly smaller family size of educated mothers in
Jordan: the higher the educational attainment of the mother, the
smaller her family size. For these and related reasons, it was argued,
women need to organize themselves to improve their position in society
and politics.

EDUCATION AND EMPLOYMENT

Because most countries in this region have high fertility and because
infant mortality has fallen dramatically, the number of school-age

children (approximately 42–45 percent of population) is increasing rapidly and will continue to do so for a number of years in the future. Jordan, for example, has compulsory schooling for the first 9 years of school, and there is some sentiment to increase it to 12 years. If present high fertility remains constant, however, the number of 6-year-old children—the group admitted to first grade—will increase by 44 percent by 1981, and the number in the 6–14 age group will increase by 47 percent. Jordan already invests a large proportion of its budget in education, and it will be increasingly difficult to provide educational facilities for children in the elementary school ages, not to mention the problem of improving the quality of education. A participant said that in Jordan's effort to provide 9 years of compulsory education, quality is sacrificed for quantity.

The failure of education to meet skill and manpower needs was mentioned in the context of burgeoning unemployment in most countries of the region. While educational expenditures absorb a large part of national budgets, inadequate attention and resources are devoted to equipping people with vocational skills. Technicians and craftsmen are in short supply in urban areas and in the growing industrial and service sectors despite increasing unemployment and underemployment in the labor force.

Participants, noting that vocational education has been neglected in the Middle East, said that it would speed development to make it much more widely available. The potential cost of vocational education, said to be several times higher than general education, is one reason for its low level. More important, however, is inertia in the educational system.

The goal of universal literacy, still far from a reality, is actively pursued in almost all countries of the Middle East. Literacy also varies widely within the region. In Afghanistan the figure for literacy is only about 8 percent, whereas in Egypt more than two thirds of males and females are counted as literate. In the overall picture of the Middle East, however, large proportions of males, and even higher proportions of females, are illiterate. This situation is changing rapidly in some countries because larger proportions of young children, both male and female, are now enrolled in school. For example, in Tunisia 96 percent of males and females of the primary-school age group are enrolled in school, and in Egypt and Turkey relatively high proportions are enrolled.

The problem presented by large numbers of school-age children has led to important innovations. In Iran it was anticipated that during the

Third Development Plan (1962–1968) the shortage of teachers would create major problems. By introducing short-term teacher-training programs and employing a large number of high school and university graduates, the problem of teacher shortage was largely overcome. Much of the increase in teaching personnel was accomplished by expanding the literacy corps, which permits young men of military age to serve as teachers in rural areas instead of undertaking conventional military service. Creation of the literacy corps was one of the revolutionary steps taken during the Third Plan. It was most effective in promoting the primary-education program and achieving a more even distribution of schools between rural and urban areas.

The magnitude of Iran's problem is illustrated by figures in the Fourth Development Plan (1968–1972). If primary education is extended during the period to include 93 percent of school-age children in towns and 55 percent in rural areas, the number of pupils will increase from 2.9 million to 3.7 million.

URBAN GROWTH

In most Middle East countries the rapid growth of urban areas, particularly capitals and other large cities, is considered an acute problem. Urban planners are confronted with shortages of housing and health services. Water is scarce in much of the region, particularly in Jordan and Iran. It was said that water scarcity will limit urban growth in the two countries, especially in Amman and Tehran. Urban employment is not expanding enough to absorb all the inmigrants: Service industries are already swollen, and unemployment and underemployment are increasing. In spite of all these constraints, rapid urban growth continues.

Several participants mentioned the need for investment and location policies to reduce growth rates in the largest cities. Some countries already have policies aimed in this direction, but the effects so far appear to be minimal—partly because these policies are recent, but also because they have not been implemented with vigor, or with sufficient funds.

Beirut, however, seems to be an exception to the general pessimism about urban growth. It has grown from 350,000 to 1,200,000 in the last 20 years, but for the most part this growth was viewed positively, because urban industry and services are responsible for higher per capita incomes in the city and contribute most to national income. The

negative aspects of rapid urbanization—crime, delinquency, anonymity—were said to be relatively unknown in Beirut until recently. This is explained in part by the city's remarkable dynamism
in attracting businesses and creating jobs and by the less rapid inmigration in recent years. A new phenomenon is a movement of population
outward to the suburbs of Beirut.

Lower fertility is typically associated with urbanization. In Turkey,
for example, it is assumed in the Third Plan (1973–1977) that as the
share of urban population increases, the growth rate of total population will decline because of lower fertility in urban areas. The figures
for Amman, Jordan, show no lower fertility there than in rural areas,
possibly reflecting the very recent refugee migration into the cities.
In a discussion of the influence of urbanization on fertility, participants
seemed to agree that modernization, rather than urbanization, is the
important determinant of fertility.

ISLAM: INCONSISTENCIES AND REINTERPRETATIONS

In most Middle East countries religious or traditional customs and
norms are major obstacles to public discussion of population policy.
Several participants took the position that Islam is often used as a convenient excuse by politicians who want to avoid making difficult
choices. Indeed, the 1971 Rabat Conference of Islamic Religious
Leaders noted that Islam and family planning are not inconsistent.
Some religious leaders at the conference argued that abortion is permitted in the first trimester and does not violate the spirit of Islam—a
view that was not expressed by the conference as a whole.

Although some seminar participants argued that on social grounds,
as well as for the health of the mother, abortion should be legalized, it
remained a topic of controversy. Abortion is a delicate matter in most
Middle East countries; to raise the issue openly may, some participants
cautioned, mobilize strong opposition. Only in Yugoslavia, Iran, and,
with some qualifications, in Tunisia has abortion been made legal. In
countries where abortion is illegal, however, it is often readily performed by medical and nonmedical personnel.

Participants noted that several well-known religious figures are now
taking a more liberal stand on family planning. In small towns, villages,
and rural areas, however, lower order leaders (such as the Mullahs in
Turkey and Iran) are not aware of the recent liberal interpretations of
religious tenets. Recently, some governments have tried to educate

religious leaders in the periphery on reinterpretations of, or changes in, traditional Islamic doctrine. In Iran, for example, a Religious Corps (similar to the Literacy Corps), created in 1971 and composed of theology students, carries the contemporary interpretation of the Koran to the villages. In Afghanistan it is possible to enroll some religious leaders to carry the family planning message to the people during the traditional Friday religious services.

Although religion poses a problem for population-policy development, participants felt that the boundaries of permissible behavior are gradually broadening, perhaps more rapidly than was previously thought possible. In some countries—notably Tunisia, Turkey, and Iran—it has been possible to enact civil laws that supersede the Koranic Code. In Turkey, for example, women have equal inheritance rights. In Iran and Tunisia polygamy is no longer permitted. On the other hand, in Lebanon, a highly commercialized society (where the average age at marriage is 23.2 years for females and 28.5 for males, a situation closer to that prevailing in the West than in most developing countries), attempts by Lebanese authorities to formulate uniform civil laws governing personal relationships have met with little success. The Personal Status Code for the various religious groups encompasses a multiplicity of laws governing personal status, marriage, divorce, inheritance, guardianship, and so forth. In 1959 the law of inheritance under the Personal Status Code was amended to give non-Moslem women equal inheritance rights with men, but this law is far from uniformly enforced.

Islamic laws can have clearly counterproductive economic and social consequences. For example, inheritance laws accord all male progeny equal rights to the father's land, a situation that has hindered land-reform efforts and fragmented landholdings into uneconomic units. In Egypt and Iran, it was necessary to organize small farmers into agricultural cooperative corporations, partly to counteract the fragmentation of arable land.

Although most participants recognized some adverse implications of Islamic law, they expressed little direct opposition to the religious code. Some spoke of the need to consolidate the changes brought about by secular laws, but, in general, they acknowledged the importance of religion. Some disagreement arose, however, on the extent to which religion is used as an excuse for not modifying the traditional order. A few said that religious tenets are sometimes consciously used to block social change.

FOREIGN AID

Toward the end of the seminar, discussion turned to the question of foreign aid. In several countries aid from both private and government organizations was valuable in the initial stages of establishing family-planning programs and providing supplies and services long before official views became sympathetic. This initial help sustained the interest and dedicated efforts of small private groups. In Tunisia the contribution of foreign assistance to the official family-planning program was, and is, major.

Foreign advisers have played a crucial role in family planning and providing expertise for census-taking and demographic studies. It was also said that it has sometimes been useful to have foreign advisers initially help a government prepare a report on the population-policy needs of the country. If the report or parts of it are politically unacceptable, it is easier to reject it because it was prepared by outsiders.

Increasingly, however, the attitude toward foreign funding, particularly bilateral aid, is becoming less enthusiastic. National planning agencies do not understand why funds are readily available for family planning and other directly related activities but not for sectors or projects that they consider vital to the nation's economic progress. In countries with Palestinian refugees, the ready availability of funds for family planning from some Christian church groups, given the plight of these refugees, is also suspect.

It was agreed that multilateral aid from international organizations is more acceptable because their motives are less questionable.

Population policy should be defined and formulated in each country, without regard to the availability of foreign funds. The need for coordination among various agencies offering assistance was illustrated by a participant who said that in Iran one village of fewer than 200 inhabitants had been subjected to the ministrations of 17 different agencies engaged in programs to improve its lot.

The participants in this seminar reflected an especially strong sensitivity to the issues that surround modernization, or the changing of traditional values, in societies whose culture is dominated by the tenets of a powerful religion. Substantial attention and discussion were devoted to ways of introducing change, particularly with reference to fertility limitation, and to the problems of setting the stage for women to achieve equal status in society.

PARTICIPANTS

MR. ABUDULLAH ALI, Director, The Arab Institute for Economic and Social Planning, Kuwait City, Kuwait

DR. JURAJ ANDRASSY, Professor, Law Faculty, University of Zagreb, Zagreb, Yugoslavia

MR. WASEF YACOUB AZAR, Researcher, Royal Scientific Society, Amman, Jordan

DR. SAYED ABDUL KADER BAHA, Adviser, Prime Ministry, Royal Government of Afghanistan, Kabul, Afghanistan

MRS. KATJA BOH, Senior Researcher, Institute of Sociology, University of Ljubljana, Ljubljana, Yugoslavia

DR. DUSAN BREZNIK, Director, Demographic Research Center, Institute for Social Sciences, Belgrade, Yugoslavia

MME. SOUAD CHATER, Sous Directeur au Ministere de la Sante Publique, Bab Saadoun, Tunis, Tunisia

DR. HALUK CILLOV, Co-Director, Institute of Statistics, Faculty of Economics, University of Istanbul, Beyazil-Istanbul, Turkey

DR. SADI CINDORUK, Department of Economics and Statistics, Orta Dogu Teknik Universiti (Middle East Technical University), Ankara, Turkey

MR. ALI HAMDI EL-GAMMAL, Managing Editor, *Al-Ahram*, Cairo, Arab Republic of Egypt

MISS SATTAREH FARMAN-FARMAIAN, Director, Tehran School of Social Work, Tehran, Iran

DR. JAMAL K. HARFOUCHE, Chairman, Department of Community Health Practice, School of Public Health, American University of Beirut, Beirut, Lebanon

DR. SAMIR KHALAF, Research Fellow, Center for Middle Eastern Studies, Harvard University, Cambridge, Massachusetts, U.S.A. (Citizen of Lebanon)

DR. ADNAN MROUEH, Assistant Professor, Department of Obstetrics and Gynecology, American University Hospital, Beirut, Lebanon

MR. SHAHPOUR NEMAZEE, Managing Editor, *Kayhan International*, Tehran, Iran

MR. TOUFIC OSSEIRAN, Secretary General, Lebanese Family Planning Association, Beirut, Lebanon

MR. SAYED SHAFIE RAHEL, Editor-in-Chief, *The Kabul Times*, Kabul, Afghanistan

DR. HANNA RIZK, Senior Demographic Expert, United Nations Development Programme, Amman, Jordan (Citizen of Arab Republic of Egypt)

MR. MAHMUD SEKLANI, Adviser, Ministry of Economics, Tunis, Tunisia

DR. ELIAS SROUJI, Department of Pediatrics, American University Hospital, Beirut, Lebanon

MR. CHADLI TNANI, Director, National Office of Family Planning, Ministry of Health, Tunis, Tunisia

OBSERVER

PROFESSOR BORISLAV SAVIC, Faculty of Political Science, University of
  Belgrade, Belgrade, Yugoslavia

NAS–NRC INTERNATIONAL STEERING COMMITTEE AND STAFF

DR. NAZLI CHOUCRI, Department of Political Science, Massachusetts Institute of
  Technology, Cambridge, Massachusetts, U.S.A.; *Seminar Cochairman*
DR. W. PARKER MAULDIN, Vice President, The Population Council, New York,
  New York, U.S.A.; *Seminar Cochairman*
DR. PAVAO NOVOSEL, Faculty of Political Science, University of Zagreb,
  Zagreb, Yugoslavia; *Seminar Coordinator*
MRS. PUSHPA NAND SCHWARTZ, *Project Coordinator*
MR. W. MURRAY TODD, *Project Director*

Latin America – Commonwealth Caribbean Seminar on Population Policy

IV

Montego Bay, Jamaica, 20–24 August 1973
Association of Caribbean Universities and
Research Institutes (Jamaica)
National Academy of Sciences–National Research Council (U.S.A.)

The region encompassed by the Latin America–Commonwealth Caribbean seminar has the highest population growth rates in the world and, except for some oil-rich countries in the Middle East, the highest per capita incomes in the developing world. The predominant religion in the Latin American countries is Roman Catholicism; in the Commonwealth Caribbean countries, English Protestant. The 20 participants came from Brazil, Chile, Colombia, Costa Rica, Jamaica, Mexico, Peru, and Trinidad and Tobago. For a summary of demographic data, see Table 4.

Participants stressed that to understand the population problems and policies of Latin America, one must know that the area is in the throes of profound change. The changes to which they referred are not those of the traditional demographic variables of fertility, mortality, and spatial distribution (although such changes are taking place), but of ideological ferment and institutional upheaval. Commonwealth Caribbean participants said that in the islands there is an undercurrent of social unrest and deep concern about the role of small and newly independent nations. One participant said, ". . . we are conducting this discussion in a time of crisis."

Vast differences exist among the countries in their approaches to modernization and development, and strong and conflicting tides and countercurrents run within countries. Participants alluded to the differences in regimes and strategies for change among their countries, citing the social and political forces that create tensions at several levels of society. For example, there is the conflict between the traditionally Latin "masculine" culture and the spreading interest in and concern for the emancipation of women, the conflict between traditional Latin sexual morality and the alleged immorality believed to be associated with the widespread use of contraceptives in other regions of the world, the shift from the extended to the nuclear family, and the rapidly changing class structure as the middle class grows larger, and, finally, the changing relationship of an educated public with the church.

Participants expressed two ideological approaches to the problems of the region: One, close to Marxism, stressed the need for profound change in social structures; the other believed that problems could be solved by necessary modifications within the existing social system.

Because of the tangled web of disparate forces at play, the Latin American participants regard their societies as unusually complex. It is hoped that whatever change is attempted will benefit all strata of society materially and spiritually.

PERCEPTIONS OF POPULATION PROBLEMS

Except for the Caribbean island nations, Costa Rica, and some of the other Central American countries, population size per se is not now a problem. Spatial distribution of the population is. The combination of high fertility, low gross national product, and uneven distribution of income was seen as the essential development problem, though some participants considered fertility to be of secondary importance.

In their informal memoranda before the seminar, the participants inventoried the problems associated with high fertility and rapid population growth: the preponderance of people under 15 years of age, the heavy burden on the relatively few economically productive members of society; highly unequal income distribution; lack of teachers and educational facilities for the school-age population; a steady flow of migrants from rural to urban areas, creating marginal urban areas and marginal workers; inadequate health care in rural and many urban environments; and excessive unemployment and underemployment. Other related problems included the need for trained personnel, the effects of antiquated land-tenure laws, the overstructuring of bureaucratic organizations and planning, and ineffective implementation of stated

TABLE 4 Eight Latin America–Commonwealth Caribbean Countries: Recent Population Data

Country	Estimated Population Mid-1960 (millions)	Estimated Population, 1-1-73 (millions)	Births per 1,000 Population, 1972	Deaths per 1,000 Population, 1972	Annual Natural Increase, 1972 (%)	Years To Double Population	Population under Age 15 (%)	Life Expectancy at Birth, 1972 (years)	Urban Population (%) 1970	Urban Population (%) 1985 Projected	Inhabitants per km², 1971	GNP per Capita at 1971 Market Prices (U.S. $)	Literate Population (%) [a]	Population per Physician (thousands)
Brazil	69.73	101.58	37	9	2.8	25	42	63	57	71	11	460	67	2.0 (1969)
Chile	7.68	9.45	25	9	1.6	43	40	63	73	83	12	760	87	2.4 (1970)[b]
Colombia	15.40	23.72	43	11	3.2	22	47	61	60	74	19	370	73	2.3 (1973)
Costa Rica	1.25	1.86	32	6	2.6	27	44	69	36	42	35	590	89	1.8 (1970)
Jamaica	1.63	1.95	34	7	2.7	26	46	70	38	51	173	720	82	3.0 (1970)
Mexico	36.05	54.96	43	9	3.4	20	48	64	57	67	26	700	76	1.4 (1969)
Peru	10.03	14.49	41	11	3.0	23	44	58	51	59	11	480	68	1.9 (1968)
Trinidad and Tobago	0.83	1.04	24	7	1.7	41	41	69	50	66	184	940	95	2.3 (1968)

[a]Various years, 1965–1973.
[b]Ministry of Health Personnel only.
SOURCES: See Table 2, p. 8.

policies. All these problems were talked about, but most were set aside in favor of discussion of migration and marginal urban development.

To some participants, urban growth provided a much needed supply of labor for industrialization; others saw a growing reservoir of political power for popular participation in social restructuring; still others discussed the need to improve the conditions of life of the urban poor and the requirements for heavy investments in housing, health, education, transportation, and other city services.

In general, Caribbean participants were more worried than Latin Americans about high fertility and its effects on their national social and economic resources. They were unequivocal in their insistence on the need for fertility limitation in conjunction with maternal and child health care, expansion of literacy, the provision of social welfare measures, and more employment opportunities—all to be implemented within a decade or so.

Almost all the participants viewed population questions as integral, but subsidiary, to economic and social development; population is but one variable in development. They seemed to agree that the demographic transition is under way in some parts of the region, but it differs from the way it occurred in the developed countries. Once this rather abstract understanding was reached, opinions diverged on the effects of population change on development. Among the views expressed by different participants were the following:

1. In many Latin American countries a larger population would help development, because it would provide larger markets for locally manufactured products and make possible a more effective exploitation of natural resources, including land, water, energy, forests, and minerals.

2. In several Central American and Caribbean countries a smaller population would be helpful to development because it would reduce the pressure on resources, including land, water, capital, and infrastructure.

3. Rapid population growth, in contrast to absolute population size or density, is a serious impediment to development because it entails larger dependency burdens, pressures for more jobs for the rapidly growing labor force, and pressures on education and other social services.

4. With the possible exception of rapid urbanization, the macroeconomic effects of population changes, including rapid population growth, on development are fairly small.

5. Regardless of possible macroeconomic effects, reducing family size among the poor would improve family welfare and, therefore, in itself be one kind of social development. The benefits to family welfare would include increased freedom for mothers and couples, greater opportunities for employment of women outside the home, better nutrition and health of children, and greater educational opportunities for children.

SPECTRUM OF DEVELOPMENT POLICIES

The spectrum of development policies discussed ranged from those that emphasize the growth of gross national product to those that emphasize income redistribution. The two approaches are described in a broad outline:

Option 1   Primary concentration on rapid increase of gross national product characterized by

- A high level of capital investment in manufacturing industry;
- Manipulation of agricultural and industrial prices resulting in a drain of capital from rural areas for use in industrial development;
- Use of "modern" capital-intensive, labor-saving industrial technology to increase productivity and to encourage the multiplier effects of modern industry;
- Development of industrialization through import-substitution and export-promoting policies; expansion of state functions and capabilities;
- Development of heavy industry and manufacture of consumer durables, such as automobiles, thereby reducing external dependence;
- A rapid rise in incomes of the small segment of the population involved in the "modern" sector, including the middle and upper classes and unionized labor; and
- Most benefits going to large urban populations with relative stagnation in rural areas and smaller cities and towns.

Option 2   Primary concentration on a more equitable distribution of income and welfare among the entire population, through provision of one or more of the following:

- Better health service for both urban and rural populations;
- Widely dispersed education facilities;
- Increased number of jobs;
- Rural development;
- Improved communications;

- Increased opportunities for education and employment for women;
- Wider popular participation in decision making;
- Tax and other income-redistribution policies; and
- Family-planning programs in rural areas and among the urban poor.

Actual development policies in most countries include elements of both approaches. To some extent the emphasis placed on each option is a question of timing. In Brazil and Mexico growth has now proceeded to where more emphasis can be placed on equitable distribution of income and welfare.

POPULATION-RELATED POLICIES

The difficulty of defining population policies arose early in the discussion and persisted throughout. It was generally agreed that most population policies are normative; that is, they describe what should be. An operational definition that seemed acceptable was that a population policy exists when the public sector takes a stance vis-à-vis mortality, fertility, or spatial distribution. Throughout the discussion, participants insisted that any such policy must be part of a country's general development policy.

Both population-responsive and population-influencing policies* tend to be neglected and may, in any case, be ineffective when development strategy concentrates on a rapid increase in gross national product. Population policies can be an important component of a development strategy directed at a more equitable distribution of income and welfare. Even here, however, social, traditional, or religious constraints may result in ineffective policies to reduce fertility, or prevent or delay introduction of such policies.

In some countries, such as Colombia, efforts to reduce fertility among the poor may be thought of, at least in part, as a complement to welfare-distribution policies: By reducing rates of growth of the numbers of poor people, the costs of improving their welfare could be substantially lowered over the long term. The difficulty is that much of the effect on costs will not be significant within less than 10–20 years.

*For a definition of population-responsive and population-influencing policies, see pages 86–87.

On the question of how much time is left to solve population problems, the Latin Americans did not share the popular view from the developed nations that the "limits to growth" may be rapidly approaching. Deliberation in manipulating popular emotions and beliefs was considered critical before undertaking policy actions or changes. And action must be consistent with the prevailing political and ideological beliefs.

Although prevalence of illegal abortion was known to be the reason for the expansion of family-planning services in Chile, the reason is not compelling enough to induce most other countries in the region to follow Chile's lead. Traditional and religious values are strong, and even medically necessary abortion is legalized in only a few countries (e.g., Jamaica). There are, however, strong indications that women in the cities of Brazil, Colombia, Mexico, and other countries are increasingly resorting to illegal abortion. To prevent the serious medical problems resulting from abortion without medical supervision—and a further increase in its practice—medical and religious authorities in several countries are quietly urging private and government authorities to provide more conception-control services to prevent unwanted pregnancies.

In some countries population policies aimed at reducing growth rates exist and are acknowledged: Costa Rica, Colombia, Trinidad and Tobago, and Jamaica. It is significant that in each country the medical profession led in the development and execution of fertility-limiting measures, first, via private institutional arrangements and, later, in conjunction with national authorities. In other countries population policies were instituted with other objectives. For example, Brazil's development policy for relatively undeveloped parts of the country includes policies to increase population and investment in these areas.

It was emphasized that population policy, as well as other policies, generally serve the interests and reflect the values of the power elite within each country. If policies are to be beneficial to the great mass of the population, they must be more responsive to the needs of all the people, and this must involve a new process of participation by the masses.

WOMEN AND THE FAMILY

The need to improve the status of women via increased education and employment was illustrated by a case history of a typical rural girl who on reaching the age of 14 or 15 has no alternative but marriage and family. She moves from "subjugation" by father and brothers to subjugation by her husband. She has no other horizons and no training or education to equip her for any career other than immediate motherhood.

Other young women, finding themselves in this situation, "escape" to urban areas where they accept low-paid service, industrial or domestic work, or they even fall into prostitution. Without knowledge of birth control practices, many become pregnant and are victims of hazardous induced abortion.

Male officials often do not understand women's needs. For example, with improved health conditions in Jamaica, many women have had all the children they want by age 25. Not at ease with contraceptives, many wish to be sterilized. Their request, however, meets with resistance by male health service doctors who are unable to comprehend the compelling desire of these women to free themselves of additional pregnancies or reliance on unfamiliar contraceptives.

Labor laws that theoretically protect women from hardship and exploitation sometimes have the effect of denying them equal job opportunities. Equal pay and career advancement are denied to women, and laws guaranteeing equality have not proved to be effective. Enforcement is not easy, given machismo in Latin American culture and the sociocultural tolerance of existing inequalities in the Caribbean region.

On the extraordinarily difficult problem of creating equal job opportunities for women when there are not enough jobs for unemployed and underemployed men, participants agreed that in most countries of the region jobs are not created fast enough to absorb new male jobseekers each year. One participant said that it is difficult to speak of raising the status of women in society when a man lacks self-respect and dignity because he cannot earn enough regularly to support a woman and their children. This was cited as one reason for "visiting" relationships in the Caribbean countries.

Participants from both Latin American and Caribbean countries discussed the extent of "illegitimacy" and stressed that this term must be understood in a regional context. Common law marriages and visiting relationships can and often do provide a certain amount of family stability and economic security; nevertheless, the maternal family is prevalent throughout the area. Although paternity and maintenance laws state that men are responsible for child support, these laws are hard to enforce. It was agreed that stricter enforcement would result in more responsible parenthood on the part of both partners. In some Latin American cities, abandoned or neglected children constitute a disturbing problem.

ROLE OF THE CATHOLIC CHURCH

In a discussion of existing population policies in Latin America the role of the Roman Catholic Church cannot be ignored. This complex subject, as revealed by the participants, defies easy attempts at generalization. Participants from different countries had different views of the role of the church, and individual opinions from the same country differed, apparently according to political, economic, and moral perspectives.

Two themes were visible in the complicated and involved discussions of the church's role: First, the church is a powerful cultural institution that has influenced both economic and social history as profoundly as it has affected individual behavior; however, it is not a monolithic institution, and church representatives hold a variety of opinions. Second, it was recognized that the political influence of the church on the organs of government is quite different in character and comprehensiveness from its influence on the lives of individuals.

Participants agreed that the church is now taking some positive stands on the concept of "responsible parenthood." This seems to mean different things depending on the country and the context, but it generally includes legitimacy and parental support, which can be regarded as part of the web of ideas constituting responsible parenthood. It is also beginning to stand for limiting fertility and spacing births.

To some, the church is identified with the "ruling classes," and most agreed that the church in its cultural tradition has fostered an acceptance of centralized political power and paternalistic rule.

Some participants saw the church as an institution that rejects "external pressure" on the individual or the couple, and on the medical and nursing professions. Stressing the importance of individual decisions, based on informed opinion and education, the church has opposed what it deems "coercive psychological tactics" on the part of people and institutions, many from outside the region.

FOREIGN AID

Deep suspicion of both bilateral and multilateral aid was revealed in the discussion of the role of foreign agencies in population and population-related problems. The theory that a dollar spent on birth control is more effective than a dollar invested in development projects was forcefully rejected. International and bilateral assistance must coincide with the priorities a country establishes for itself.

In general, foreign institutions (the U.S. Agency for International Development, World Bank, International Planned Parent Federation, etc.) were criticized for "putting on blinkers," for being too narrow in approach, and failing to give due attention to recipient countries' goals. They are seen as giving money away "according to their own rules." Multilateral agencies are, according to several participants, becoming highly politicized and bureaucratically homogenized. Private or public, national or multilateral, small or large, most aid-giving agencies today are seen to operate in the same way, giving the appearance of having common criteria for financing and funding projects and programs. They are believed to dictate solutions and terms with great rigidity. Moreover, they are subject to fads that sweep the developed countries that they bring to the developing countries; witness, it was said, the plethora of funds available today for population and environmental matters.

A call was made for wider regional and international cooperation and participation to counter the influence of a handful of powerful countries and institutions that now control funds.

POLICY OPTIONS

Different participants summarized various influences that may induce the government of a particular country to adopt a policy of fertility reduction:

1. International public opinion, particularly in the developed countries, as expressed through intergovernmental and nongovernmental organizations and bilateral governmental relations, with either positive or negative effects;

2. The belief of many leaders of public opinion in the country that reducing fertility and rates of population growth will lower one serious barrier to economic and social development;

3. Pressure from groups such as physicians and social welfare workers concerned with maternal and child health and family welfare;

4. The belief of some elite groups within the country that fertility control will lower the pressures for radical social and economic change.

Toward the last day of the seminar participants were asked to comment on some practical responses to hypothetical courses of action suggested earlier and on a few of the more widely held notions prevalent among groups outside the region. The following questions were briefly discussed within the time available.

1. What feasible population-responsive policies would have the most population-influencing effects?
- A radical change in the educational system?
- Removal of employment discrimination against women?
- Making new land available to peasants?
- Intensification of agricultural production on lands now cultivated?
- Provision of more adequate health services?
- Labor-intensive industrialization to reduce unemployment?
- Other population-responsive policies?

2. How can development and population policy and planning be integrated into an overall national policy and plan? How can the administration and execution of these two kinds of policy be better coordinated?

3. In what ways would better theories of fertility and migratory behavior and better models of development have a significant influence on population policy? What would be the effect of more accurate and complete demographic and other statistical data?

4. Would a more widespread appreciation of the effects of rapid population growth among government leaders, journalists, university faculty members, the military, and other influential, powerful groups be useful in creating and carrying out more effective population policies or in developing collaboration in these policies?

The response of the Latin American participants was strong. About the first question, for example, one participant stated that emphasis should be given to all the possible courses offered with the goal of improving the people's lot and only secondarily to reducing fertility.

The response from the Caribbean participants was more pragmatic: How do you do these things, and how do you set priorities among them? They voiced a certain skepticism about multiple efforts, followed by a paucity of publicized evaluations of these efforts.

It was generally agreed that social and economic development policies that improve the welfare of the poorer half of the population will have a significant effect on fertility and may even be a prerequisite for fertility reduction. Certain income-distribution policies—greater employment opportunities for women and a higher average level of education—may be more effective than others in reducing fertility but less effective in promoting the overall goals of economic and social development. How resources should be allocated to different welfare-distribution policies is not obvious without greater understanding of their effects on both fertility and development.

Several hypotheses regarding the effects of policies were advanced.

• A more equal distribution of income will result in a decrease in fertility and rural–urban migration.

• Creation of stable employment in marginal areas will reduce fertility and reduce migration.

• More widely available health, education, and housing services will influence fertility and reduce migration.

• Increased participation of marginal groups in influencing political action, a higher status for women, and equitable land redistribution will have a negative effect on fertility and migration.

In answer to question 2 on the integration of development and population policies, it was generally agreed that social and economic development must be given priority. This raised several basic issues.

As formulated by one participant:

• Given a development policy, what may be the demographic consequences of the policy?

• Will the demographic consequences advance or retard development?

• If they advance development, can we take steps to augment the positive demographic effects?

• If they do not advance development, can we take steps to counteract the negative effects?

• What resources are available under the development plan?

• What complementary measures can be introduced?

He went on to describe the formulation of population-influencing policies as including these necessary first steps:

1. Greater understanding among policymakers and national planning agencies of the consequences of rapid population growth on the welfare of the majority of the population;

2. At the same time, greater understanding of the effects of different kinds of improvements in welfare on fertility;

3. Identification and definition of welfare policies, including family-planning services, that can be expected to affect fertility; and

4. Comparative analysis of the overall benefits and costs of these and other welfare policies as a basis for allocating government resources.

Comments on the need for removing discrimination against women in employment and education revealed strong appreciation that female employment in nontraditional sectors and education of females have a fertility-dampening effect, as well as an element of social justice.

Question 4, about expanding the appreciation of the effects of rapid population growth among political and opinion leaders, drew this reply: Such educational efforts frequently result in a negative response, an overreaction, and then a systematic rejection. Implicit in this comment was the belief that opinion leaders are likely to consider discussion of the consequences of rapid population growth as propaganda from the North, to be rejected as such, whether true or false.

At the end of the seminar it was agreed that the style of development on which a country is embarked sets the tone and pace for specific policies and, therefore, the projects. Furthermore, the goals of individuals and of countries are not and should not be identical.

PARTICIPANTS

T. S. GUADALUPE AGUILAR FERNANDEZ, Directora, Escuela de Trabajo Social Vasco de Quiroga, México, D. F., México

DR. NORMA ANDREWS, Medical Consultant, Population Programme, Ministry of Health, Port of Spain, Trinidad and Tobago

DR. CANDIDO PROCOPIO FERREIRA DE CAMARGO, Director, Centro de Estudos de Dinâmica Populacional, Universidade de São Paulo, Faculade de Saúde Pública, São Paulo, Brasil

DR. RAMIRO DELGADO, Director, International Program, Family Health Foundation, New Orleans, Louisiana, U.S.A.

DR. AMAURY DE SOUZA, Instituto Universitário de Pesquisas do Rio de Janeiro, Botafogo, Rio de Janeiro, Brasil

DR. GERARDO GONZALEZ CORTES, Jefe del Sector Políticas de Población, Centro Latinoamericano de Demografía, Universidad de Chile, Santiago de Chile, Chile

SRTA. FANNY GONZALEZ FRANCO, Magistrada Sala Laboral, Tribunal Superior, Manizales, Colombia

PADRE AFONSO GREGORY, Centro de Estatística Religiosa e Investigações Sociais, Rio de Janeiro, Brasil

PADRE GUSTAVO JIMENEZ C., Provincia Colombiana, S.J., Vice Provincial Socio-Pastoral, Bogotá D.E., Colombia

SR. RICARDO JIMENEZ J., Director Ejecutivo, Centro de Estudios Sociales y de Población, Universidad de Costa Rica, Ciudad Universitaria "Rodrigo Facio," Costa Rica

DR. RICARDO LAGOS, Secretario General, Facultad Latinoamericana de Ciencias Sociales, Santiago, Chile

DR. JORGE MENDEZ MUNEVAR, Integración y Desarrollo, Bogotá, Colombia

DR. WYNANTE PATTERSON, Medical Director, National Family Planning Board, Kingston, Jamaica

DR. JOSEPH RAJBANSEE, Senior Lecturer, Department of Government, University of West Indies, Mona, Kingston, Jamaica (Citizen of Guyana)

DR. PEDRO REYES ORTEGA, Profesor de Econometría, El Colegio de México, México, D.F., México

SR. DIEGO ROBLES RIVAS, Arquitecto, Director, Adjunto *Sinamos*, Dirección General de Pueblos Jóvenes, Areas de Sub-Desarrollo, Urbano Interno, Centro Cívico, Lima, Perú

SR. ALEJANDRO RODRIGUEZ Y GONZALEZ, Arquitecto, El Colegio de México, México, D.F., México

DR. ERNESTO SCHIEFELBEIN, Director, Programa Interdisciplinario de Investigaciones en Educación, Universidad Católica de Chile, Santiago, Chile

DR. KARL SMITH, Director, Family Planning Unit, Department of Social and Preventive Medicine, University of the West Indies, Mona, Kingston, Jamaica

DR. GUILLERMO VARELA VELASQUEZ, Jefe, División Sociodemográfica, Departamento de Planeamiento Nacional, Bogotá, Colombia

REPRESENTATIVES OF COSPONSORING ORGANIZATIONS

DR. LUIS LEÑERO OTERO, Director, Instituto Mexicano de Estudios Sociales, México, D.F., México; Member, NAS–NRC International Steering Committee; *Seminar Cochairman*

DR. ROGER REVELLE, Director, Center for Population Studies, Harvard University, Cambridge, Massachusetts, U.S.A.; *ex officio* Member, NAS–NRC International Steering Committee; *Seminar Cochairman*

MRS. PUSHPA NAND SCHWARTZ, NAS–NRC, Washington, D.C., U.S.A.; *Project Coordinator*

MR. W. MURRAY TODD, NAS–NRC, Washington, D.C., U.S.A.; *Project Director*

MR. HECTOR WYNTER, Projects Director, Association of Caribbean Universities and Research Institutes, Kingston, Jamaica; *Seminar Coordinator*

African
Seminar on
Population Policy

V

Nairobi, Kenya, 10–14 September 1973
Institute for Development Studies, University of Nairobi (Kenya)
National Academy of Sciences–National Research Council (U.S.A.)

The views of a small group of Africans who agreed to discuss what is today a controversial topic in Africa are summarized here. This report should not be read as a demographic analysis of the region or as a survey of attitudes. All 21 seminar participants came from sub-Saharan countries: the People's Republic of the Congo (Brazzaville), Ethiopia, Ghana, Ivory Coast, Nigeria, Kenya, Tanzania, Uganda, and Zaire. Table 5 summarizes demographic data on these countries.

Bringing together African demographers, health and manpower administrators, journalists, leaders of women's organizations, city planners, public leaders, and economists to discuss the many aspects and ramifications of population policy on the African continent at this time carries certain risks. Africa, despite some common economic and demographic trends, defies simple description or packaged analysis. Vast numbers of African languages are spoken across a continent that contains rich and different cultural heritages, histories, and social traditions. Throughout the seminar one was reminded frequently that independence came to most countries of this region only slightly more than 10 years ago.

A collective understanding of the term "population policy" was arrived at only after considerable effort and after a recognition that some countries and parts of countries are, by their own standards and interests, underpopulated. Overcoming the notion that population

55

TABLE 5 Nine African Countries: Recent Population Data

Country	Estimated Population, Mid-1960 (millions)	Estimated Population, 1-1-73 (millions)	Births per 1,000 Population, 1972	Deaths per 1,000 Population, 1972	Annual Natural Increase, 1972 (%)	Years To Double Population	Population under Age 15 (%)	Life Expectancy at Birth, 1972 (years)	Urban Population (%) 1970	Urban Population (%) Projected 1985	Inhabitants per km², 1971	GNP per Capita at 1971 Market Prices (U.S. $)	Literate Population (%)[a]	Population per Physician (thousands)
Congo (People's Republic of)	0.77	0.99	44	21	2.3	30	41	44	31	na[b]	3	270	20	na
Ethiopia	20.70	26.95	51	25	2.6	27	45	40	9	15	23	80	5	72 (1970)
Ghana	6.78	9.81	47	18	2.9	24	46	48	31	45	37	250	25	12 (1971)
Ivory Coast	3.23	4.62	46	22	2.4	29	44	43	23	na	14	330	20	13.9 (1970)
Kenya	8.12	12.88	49	17	3.2	22	47	49	10	17	20	160	20–25	8 (1970)
Nigeria	42.91	58.15	52	25	2.7	26	45	39	23	32	61	140	25	21 (1970)
Tanzania	10.33	14.23	47	20	2.7	26	44	44	7	11	15	110	15–20	22 (1970)
Uganda	6.68	10.48	45	17	2.8	25	43	49	10	17	53	130	20	8.7 (1969)
Zaire	14.14	18.73	44	21	2.3	30	44	44	16	27	10	90	15–20	34 (1969)

[a]Various years, 1965–1973.
[b]na = not available.
SOURCES: See Table 2, p. 8.

56

policy is to be equated with family planning or fertility control was a major preoccupation of the seminar.

MAJOR THEMES

Three underlying concepts pervaded the discussions of population variables and policies: independence, the meaning of fertility to Africans, and education as a key to development.

Independence

Most participants expressed a strong desire to develop and nurture an African viewpoint on vital issues. This preoccupation manifested itself in several ways. Despite a substantial residue of antipathy toward the colonial heritage, there is positive enthusiasm for internalized decision making, self-help, and self-reliance; oversimplified solutions are rejected, and an African definition and solution to African problems are consciously sought.

Participants stressed time and again that their problems are different from those of the rest of the world and that the solutions must be found in the African context. They wish neither to accept blindly the analysis of, or solutions to, their problems offered by outsiders nor to disassociate themselves from the world approach to development. It is evident to them that the African path to development will be long and arduous; equally clear, however, is the belief that they must find their own way on that path.

Fertility

Because Africa was depopulated by slave trade, tribal warfare, and violence instigated by outsiders and because of the need to offset high mortality in many parts of the continent, fertility is highly regarded in some African societies. Some of the discussions reflected this positive attitude toward fertility. It was said that in African societies fertility is very important to the value of a married woman; in some, marriage to a barren woman is not regarded as permanent. The well-being and survival of the family, clan, ethnic group, and now the nation are thought by many to be directly related to the number of productive people. For example, under the systems of subsistence agriculture in Africa children are productive members of the family who are perceived as enhancing its economic, as well as social and psychological, well-being.

Several African countries are actively encouraging population growth, some on a nationwide basis, others in selected areas. But even in countries where fertility control and slowing the rate of population growth are either officially desired or tacitly accepted, there is some reluctance to interfere with fertility too directly in the absence of alternative roles for women.

Education

The participants assigned a priority role to education. It is the key to development, which in turn is the key to solving population problems: health education to improve nutrition and sanitation, maternal and child care; vocational education to improve agriculture, stimulate industrialization, and increase management and manpower resources; general education to free women from their traditional roles and to make society more egalitarian; sex and family-life education to teach children how to accomodate to a rapidly changing society. Within the educational and developmental framework the problems of population change can be handled and policies can be designed, but, as one participant noted, the first goal of education must be to help people learn how to plan for a better and more secure future.

These themes have been presented here in a brief and general way. Nonetheless, they could be manifestations of powerful forces affecting African development and decision making.

PERCEPTIONS OF POPULATION PROBLEMS

At present, rapid population growth is viewed as a problem to be solved by government action in only two or three African countries that have moved, or are moving, in the direction of an official policy on fertility control and a national family-planning program. All the participants, however, detailed the difficulties their countries face in meeting planned development targets and objectives, such as increasing school enrollment and facilities to achieve universal primary education, providing health services and other social needs such as housing, and creating job opportunities adequate for new jobseekers as well as the backlog of unemployed or underemployed. Several participants expressed concern that a high proportion of dependent children creates a heavy burden on their national resources and reduces the amounts available for productive investment, but few of their governments seem ready to take action now to reduce population growth rates.

The notion that rapid population growth rates could jeopardize national development objectives is not widely accepted, and fertility control is nowhere assigned a high priority. Official emphasis is placed almost wholly on increasing the pace of national economic growth to achieve higher levels of living and, subordinately, on taking care of a growing population. The increasing rural-to-urban migration and the consequent rapid growth of one primary city or a few major cities (some of which double in population in approximately 10–12 years), however, is seen as a serious problem confronting all countries.

In much of Africa south of the Sahara—especially in areas that have, in the African context, relatively low fertility, like the People's Republic of the Congo, Gabon, and Zaire—there is a desire to increase population size. This is motivated by a desire to achieve economies of scale through increasing population densities and to have a larger domestic market. Under conditions of increasing demand for labor in subsistence and commercial agriculture and mining, a larger labor force is seen as a productive element in national development. Mortality rates have been rather high and are still about the highest in the world, although high fertility is seen as offsetting high mortality. Mortality rates, in the opinion of several participants, must be reduced if birth rates are to come down.

It was also stated that the general land : man ratio, or population density, is low in Africa compared with almost any other region of the world. Given its vast potential resources, it is presumed that Africa could easily support a much larger total population. One participant said that Africa is only now beginning to replenish its numbers, drastically reduced by violence in the past. What the new African nations, just coming into their own, need most is time to develop their strength and confidence; it is premature to "lecture" or "worry" them about population growth. The immediate concern is how to improve the quality of life of their people. Their attention and resources will be devoted mainly to reducing mortality (although declining, it is still high); improving health, nutrition, and housing; increasing educational opportunities; developing skills; and increasing national productivity.

To solve current employment problems and create greater job opportunities for their nationals, some countries in both West and East

Africa are finding it convenient to curb immigration and legislate special provisions on ownership of property and employment. Non-nationals are steadily eased out of "entrenched" and enviable positions in industry and commerce, education, and government. Such actions are consistent with the strong sense of nationalism felt and encouraged in African countries.

The question of refugee populations was alluded to in connection with the nearly 1 million refugees from the fighting in Angola who are living in Zaire and the drought-affected people in the Sahelian zone of Northwest Africa. The recent disastrous drought in this area was discussed briefly in terms of possible climatic changes and the relationship of man to resources. There was hardly any discussion of types of resource exploitation in more prosperous areas, but the concern was explicit that whatever resources exist in the continent, they should be exploited by Africans rather than "outsiders."

The question of alien control of natural resources and the complex relationships between African exporters of raw materials and developed-nation users was discussed by one participant: A most serious population problem for Africa is the child in the developed country who will consume resources several times over those consumed by an African child. The points at issue are not only the conservation of African natural resources for Africans but also the supposedly lavish use of world resources by the developed nations, which creates resource scarcities. Developed nations, it was said, hope to solve the problem not by restricting their use of resources or further reducing their rates of population growth, but by asking the developing countries to restrict their population growth.

Current population structures, distribution, and movements carry with them several problems of concern to African governments. For example, governments have to allocate more and more resources to educate an increasing number of children in the school system, which for some countries has become a heavy burden. In certain areas the population is dispersed among scanty settlements, leading to high costs for transport and communications. In other areas urbanization creates problems of providing adequate housing, sanitation, and other essential services. One further problem associated with population is creating an equitable distribution of income and services. Some participants considered social justice to be the foremost priority of African countries.

POPULATION POLICIES IN SOME NATIONS

Population was viewed as one of many problems in development—
including the adverse terms of trade that plague the African countries—
and as a problem without a single solution. Since many different
variables influence population size and growth and have different effects on the economy, particular solutions must be tailored to each
situation. Decisions on what policies should be implemented to influence population variables—such as fertility, mortality, and migration—
are made at three distinct levels (the individual, the national, and the
global), and these decisions must be coordinated.

Reducing mortality and morbidity rates was regarded as the most important goal for African countries in their population policies. As for
fertility, it was argued that socioeconomic changes, like increased education, better income distribution, and higher standards of living would
lead in the long run to lower fertility rates. Internal migration was the
subject of considerable discussion. The participants concluded that
population policy at this stage in African development should be concerned primarily with defining mortality, fertility, and migration goals
that are consistent with national objectives. These goals should then be
achieved through implementation of comprehensive national socioeconomic development policies.

Health and Mortality

The discussion on mortality indicated great dissatisfaction with the
current low priority assigned to health care in national budgets. Several
African countries, it was said, have concentrated on curative rather than
preventive medicine in their health services, and political considerations
have too often influenced the location of hospitals and health care
centers and the extension of social services.

Although detailed figures for health care expenditures were not
cited, it was the consensus of the seminar that far more effort should
be directed to maternal and child health care, preventive medicine,
sanitation, and education about nutrition and simple personal hygiene.
The results of small and simple measures, like providing clean well
water in rural areas, could bring great benefits. Reducing infant mortality through elementary nutritional education demands much more attention. Participants were greatly concerned with the extremely low
ratios of doctors and nurses to total population.

Fertility

As mentioned earlier, much of the discussion of fertility was based on the assumption that, in the long run, economic-development variables will be the fertility-controlling factors. This view seemed partly a re-action to what was described as the overselling of family planning by institutions of the developed world, but far more important was the understanding that only a general enhancement of living standards will motivate people to limit fertility.

Comments on the experience with family-planning services noted that in most countries these services are available on a limited scale through private and voluntary agencies. In Ghana and Kenya they are now more widely available through government programs. Tanzania is permitting a private program to use government facilities. Participants agreed that family-planning services should be available to all married couples so that they can space their children and have the desired number.

Traditional family-planning practices are breaking down in many urban areas, so the demand for modern contraceptives is growing with rapid urbanization and modernization. It may be timely in some coun-tries to ask if the available services and delivery systems are adequate. Some participants argued, however, that it is premature for African governments or outsiders to "push" family planning before the people, especially the women who must use such methods, are educated and express their needs. Traditional methods of child spacing, passed on from mother to daughter, are still very much in use in many African areas. In this context, it was said that the use of modern contraceptives may not be accepted by African women, especially in rural areas; it would do more harm than good to propagate their use until people are educated as to their safety and willing to accept them.

Family-planning services have been expanded so rapidly in some areas that the clinics are woefully understaffed and irregularly serviced. In Tanzania a negative reaction to family planning followed the use of (and subsequent widespread adverse publicity on) an inadequately tested hormone injection. Stiffer standards for testing and screening drugs and devices have been instituted as a result of this experience.

In answer to a concern expressed by one participant that family-planning services have been misused, that unmarried school-age girls have been known to get contraceptives from family-planning clinics, another participant replied that some misuse or defects are unavoidable in any program. Improvements are continually being made, however, to prevent such misuse. Moreover, promiscuity and other negative effects that may accompany the availability of contraceptives reflect social pressures and social change. They indicate the need for more widespread and better sex education for young people, especially in secondary schools. Young people, particularly in urban areas, need to be made aware of the consequences of irresponsible sexual behavior. In several instances sex education and family-planning services have enabled young married couples to complete their education and postpone having children.

There was general agreement that although family-planning services are needed at the individual level, they should be integrated in the health services program and, more specifically, with maternal and child welfare services. This was considered necessary for psychologic as well as economic reasons. One participant criticized foreign aid agencies for not comprehending this logic and added that their insistence on funding and setting up separate family-planning services and clinics has been most unfortunate.

The cost/benefit of fertility-control programs in other developing countries, such as India, was mentioned and used to support the argument that such programs by themselves will not alleviate the population problem. China, it was alleged, had achieved a significant drop in fertility before adopting any kind of a countrywide fertility-control program. Apparently, this drop is attributable largely to the revolutionary social and political changes in China in the last 20 years.

Participants' conclusions were that no country should undertake a fertility-control program until it feels ready and has adequate resources, human and financial, to support it. The social and economic implications of such an undertaking should be carefully studied and weighed beforehand so that, once launched, the program will not flounder for lack of commitment or adequate planning.

Migration and Urbanization

Most African governments are concerned about policies on migration, internal and external. Participants alluded to the exodus of large ethnic groups from both West and East African countries, largely resulting from policies that can be construed as economic nationalism, but did not discuss the results of these policies. Problems of internal redistribution attracted more comment and perhaps were more easily discussed. Although mention was made of rural-to-rural migration (a result of increasing population pressure on the land, coupled with prevailing agricultural systems that wear out land) and of urban-to-rural movement (the result of rural industrialization), greater concern was voiced about rural-to-urban migration and its effects on people, society, and national economies.

Almost all countries in the region are confronted with problems of rapid urbanization. The steady and growing influx of poor and unskilled country folk into cities, particularly into one or two large cities, has meant a high rate of urban unemployment; squatting and substandard, makeshift housing; increased alienation; prostitution; thefts and other crimes. Many migrants find employment in the marginal sector as vendors, hawkers, or bootblacks. Others, seasonally or partially employed, depend on support from their families in rural areas until they find permanent work.

The city planners among the participants discussed the present largely experimental or piecemeal attempts to raise housing standards and improve migrant skills. Unfortunately, these solutions are not cheap, and there is no promise that they will be sufficient to the task. Public housing and sanitation standards are generally pitched too high for immigrants to afford. Training centers are inadequate in meeting the needs for skill development. Meanwhile, the economic opportunities and the attractions of city life continue to bring in a steady stream of unskilled migrants. The situation becomes more critical each year.

A description of the Tanzanian experiment in attempting to halt the drift to urban areas and to keep the population in the villages offered a new perspective on population distribution. A few years ago the government nationalized all landholdings and began introducing a socialistic pattern of agriculture. Everyone able to work is supposed to be employed, and the education system has been redesigned for the needs of a largely rural population. The government places major emphasis on improving agricultural output, growing nutritious foods, and making villages self-sufficient. The policies applied by the Tanzanian government were said to have stabilized rural–urban population and reduced migration to the cities. High government officials and political leaders are encouraged to work in villages alongside the people and to demonstrate the importance of agriculture to a nation seeking self-sufficiency.

Participants expressed concern that some policies to control internal migration and distribution might violate personal freedom and individual human rights. The idea of passcards and residence permits, for example, was forcefully rejected.

Kenya, Nigeria, and Ghana have policies to create growth centers in rural areas, which would become a secondary or tertiary hierarchy of urban centers. Incentives are given to industries to locate outside the existing large urban centers and in newly developed centers. Rural training centers are being built in some countries. Kenya is experimenting with village "polytechnics" to complement the needs of small-scale rural industry. Such rural industry, part of a newly planned approach to rural development, is also designed to reduce the flow of people to the two major cities, Nairobi and Mombasa. This scheme is devised to create a hierarchy of service centers (health, educational, market, financial, cultural) and to link them by a communications network to permit easy access. Government funds are available to entrepreneurs to stimulate their investments, and government agencies subsidize the development of these centers. Attempts have also been made at resettlement schemes in Nigeria and Ghana, but the results of these policies are uneven or disappointing.

Some participants said that there is a good deal of talk about expanding services and creating infrastructure in smaller towns and rural areas, but in reality little money is allocated or spent. This situation is due to the previous structure and direction of investments and development decisions.

STATUS OF WOMEN

African cultures stress the role of women as wives and mothers; among the educated, however, awareness is growing that alternative roles should be provided through education and increased employment in the modern sector of the economy. Participants favored policies that will improve the status of women, increase their participation in public life, and offer alternatives to early marriage and motherhood. To some these changes are preconditions for the acceptance of family-size limitation achieved through modern fertility-control techniques.

The question of a growing female labor force facing an unemployed or underemployed male labor force in the modern sector of the economy was not discussed. Improvement in the status of women and its consequent expected increase in the age of marriage were regarded as desirable objectives, but there was little discussion of specific ways to translate these hopes into reality. Educational opportunities, particularly in elementary schools, are rapidly becoming equal for females, but for higher education—vocational, academic, or adult—little government initiative is seen on the horizon.

The changing role of women in Chinese society was mentioned. Women in China, it was said, are completely integrated into the work force at all levels; they marry later and find having large families incompatible with their outside work. Through improved educational opportunities they have been able to improve the quality of their own lives and that of their families. There is marked improvement in the nutrition, health, and sanitation of their households.

In Ghana, government policy to improve and equalize opportunities for women in education and employment was enunciated as a major policy recommendation in the 1969 Official Population Policy Statement. In Tanzania, where a major social and economic transformation is under way, the policy is for women to obtain equal access to schooling and work at all levels. The impact of these policies on fertility remains to be seen. Tanzanian schools emphasize improving nutrition, health, and sanitation practices in daily life; girls are exposed to their importance early in their schooling.

Several participants took a strong position against abortion, arguing that it is morally unacceptable, given the values of their societies and cultures. Children are highly prized by African families; some participants stressed that they are welcome even when born out of wedlock. In the African village other members of the family or friends love and provide for such children collectively.

In most countries in this region abortion is illegal or allowed only on medical grounds. Some participants, however, favored liberal abortion laws on humanitarian and health grounds and in light of the increasing incidence of illegal abortion, particularly in urban areas. Abortion, it was said, is a frequent resort after contraceptive failure. In Ghana the Law Reform Committee is studying the question of whether the abortion law should be liberalized and is thoroughly canvassing public opinion on this issue. Ethiopia, Nigeria, and the sub-Saharan Francophone countries have strong religious and cultural biases against liberalization of abortion laws and its practice as a birth control measure.

FOREIGN AID

Official aid-giving agencies, bilateral and multilateral, were criticized for being too rigid and often wrong in propagandizing their pet solutions to

African problems. Governments were cautioned against tempting "aid offers" that have led some countries to start programs that they were not able to continue on a self-supporting basis when the aid ceased or was substantially reduced.

One participant said that foreign aid agencies need to be educated on the particular needs and conditions prevailing in Africa. Another cited the case of an African government that was pressured into producing a policy on fertility control. Insistence on explicit goals of fertility reduction as a condition for aid is not acceptable to most governments because they have internal political reasons for avoiding such explicit targets.

The consensus was that African countries must set their own priorities, do more for themselves, and learn from each other and from other developing countries. Some participants voiced their suspicion that the ready availability of foreign funds for fertility control in the form of family-planning programs indicates the desire of richer countries to keep them in a weak and dependent position. Questions of dependence and unfavorable terms of trade were raised, along with a caution against attempts by rich countries to "manipulate" or "confuse" Africans by raising the spectre of environmental degradation and pollution.

The work of private agencies such as the International Planned Parenthood Federation, Pathfinder Fund, and the Population Council was acknowledged as beneficial in countries that have asked for some limited help to begin family-planning programs as a part of health services or to find out what their population problems might be through surveys, censuses, and the like.

MAKING POLICY WORK

Because this seminar included several government officials and planners, the discussion of policymaking and administration was lively. They agreed that population policies should be integrated into socio-economic planning and their administration made part of the normal plan-implementation process. To help them in this process, however, the types of data needed for such planning should be clarified. Information on crude birth and death rates, projections of the population by age and sex and by sectors (e.g., labor force, school-age group) would be most useful. Information is also required on economic indicators and trends; it could be combined with better census statistics and population projections to make possible more realistic planning in health, education, urban growth, manpower training and utilization, and indus-

trial location. Such information will require a well-conceived, contin-
uous, and directed research program on population, some of it applied
research that can be integrated into the decision-making process.

The difficulties in achieving a data base for policy are profound.
Collection of data, it was said, is substantially influenced by how local
leaders perceive the use of the data; well-known cases of town and
district population figures artificially inflated to acquire population-
based, government-financed services were cited in some detail. The difficulties of census enumeration and acquisition of birth and mortality
data, as well as the political pressures associated with the use of data,
were mentioned, with few suggestions for remedies.

It was not clear whether participants felt that some governmental
irresponsibility in this field is inevitable or that worrying about it is
pointless until data collection and analytical competence are of sufficient technical sophistication and reliability to make an independent
census feasible. In either case, it was evident that current data and existing planning capacity left the administrators in the group with grave
misgivings about the ease with which population policy formulation
can be integrated with other elements of development planning.

The most obvious problem areas, as mentioned previously, were education and urban growth. Both the technical shortcomings in education
and urban planning and the manifestations of political influence were
causes for concern. Numerous instances of locating schools, hospitals,
and health centers for political advantage and the usual proximity of
services to towns and urban centers where officials live were cited as
evidence of maladministration. It was said, for example, that in Nigeria
many schools had to be closed because they did not have enough pupils
to justify the staff and maintenance costs. The consolidation of student
bodies and the economies of concentrating teachers have eventually
outweighed the political attraction of a school in every village.

This led to a debate on the responsibility of the public servant (the
bureaucrat), compared with the responsibility of the elected or politically appointed official. Continuing arguments about the ethical responsibility for formulation and execution of government directives, it
was said, seem endemic in countries with parliamentary systems and of
far less concern in those with single party, executive rule. Nevertheless,
this issue was regarded as germane in all countries, considering the
somewhat fluid nature of most governments and the ever-present possibility that any government may move from one form to another on
little notice.

The difficult question was raised of how policy relevant to the
needs of people is to be made by the privileged elites who are also the

policymakers. The success of public policies, especially in countries where the population is firmly tradition bound, should be measured by their impact on peasant attitudes. Unless policies can be proved to benefit the peasants and help to alter their presumed traditional, fatalistic thinking, peasants will continue to see national government planning, which more often than not has proposed unsuccessful or only marginally better solutions to their problems, as interference that is irrelevant to their needs. This was declared to be the challenge for policymakers in all developing societies.

Evaluation of government policy and programs was recognized as essential to policy review. Evaluation could take place at the national, program-support, or service-delivery level where the effects of the variable being studied or influenced are measured. Evaluation has been neglected either because personnel to do the task are in short supply or because the results of policies are not easy to measure. Development planners and policymakers were strongly urged to remedy this situation.

POLICY CONSTRAINTS

Participants detailed a wide range of conditions and limitations to policy formulation and implementation. The obvious limitation of re-sources loomed large. It was agreed that the public had heard too many statements of good intentions and seen too little follow-through; it would be better to eschew policy statements or high-sounding proc-lamations without the means to make them realities for the people.

Another major limiting factor, as noted before, is the lack of accurate, complete data on population and other social and economic variables. Projections based on scanty sample surveys have often proved erroneous and have led to some costly policy mistakes.

Policy is difficult to administer in most developing countries because most people live in villages that are widely dispersed, difficult to reach, and therefore costly to service. Existing programs in education, health, and other social services cannot be carried out in all parts of a country because of lack of personnel. This difficulty is compounded by the attraction of work in developed countries for the small number of highly skilled personnel.

A serious constraint is the extremely small number of skilled and experienced administrators who can identify needs and devise novel ways to meet them. Governments are forced to hire expatriates to fill this gap, a solution very unsatisfactory to most.

The need to devise new systems in education and in medical and health training is increasingly apparent in most countries. Existing institutions and facilities based on traditional Western models are not suited to African conditions; they are costly and reach only a few. There is a serious need to invent simple technological solutions and less-capital-intensive methods for development projects and for improving daily living conditions.

Cultural and institutional parameters—traditions, religions, and local, tribal, or regional interests—circumscribe the policymaker's alternatives and make his task more difficult. Devising policies that will work within these parameters and convincing the people—including peasants—of their benefits depend on the imagination, tact, and political skill of African leaders.

It is necessary to distinguish between the constraints on policy formulation and constraints on policy execution. In policy formulation the cultural concerns, class domination, and ethnic rivalries play important roles. In the execution phase, the key factors are the absence of an educated body politic, the newness of rational planning in the lives of people, and the locus of decision making.

This last element, the locus of decision making, was not fully explored. Several participants stressed the need for Africans to take responsibility for their own destiny at each level of decision making—individual, national, and global. An obvious limit on an individual's role in policy decision and execution is his or her ability to participate in the modern world. An equally obvious constraint on the nation's policy formulation and execution is its capacity to finance policy decisions and programs. And the role of Africa in the community of nations depends on the ability of the countries of the region to act in concert.

The sense of communal responsibility in African villages was considered a resource that has not been tapped. This possibly unique cultural pattern leads to sharing land, children, and responsibility for education of one's own and other's youngsters. It has not, in most cases, been channeled into constructive collective efforts to provide the services villages desperately need, which they could create for themselves if organized to do so, perhaps with modest government help. Such needs include schoolhouses, health center buildings, roads, markets, and sanitary water supplies.

The source of initiative to act was a theme that ran from the immediate need for villagers to help themselves through bootstrap collective efforts to the question of whether African nations could conserve and husband their raw materials in a world dominated by resource-hungry developed nations.

PARTICIPANTS

PROFESSOR AMA ATA AIDOO, Department of English, University of Cape Coast, Cape Coast, Ghana

DR. ALULA ABATE, Chairman, Department of Geography, Haile Sellassie I University, Addis Ababa, Ethiopia

MR. BONGOMA KONI BOTOKE, Bureau du Recteur, Universite Nationale du Zaire, Kinshasa, Zaire

MISS HELENE BOUBOUTOU, Professor of Geography, Brazzaville, People's Republic of the Congo

MR. JEAN BOUKEI, Sous-Directeur de Statistique Generale, Abidjan, Ivory Coast

DR. K. T. DE GRAFT-JOHNSON, Deputy Director, Institute of Statistical, Social and Economic Research, University of Ghana, Legon, Ghana

DR. FECADU GADAMU, Head, Department of Sociology and Anthropology, Haile Sellassie I University, Addis Ababa, Ethiopia

DR. SAMUEL K. GAISIE, Regional Institute for Population Studies, University of Ghana, Legon, Ghana

MR. NAIGZY GEBREMEDHIN, General Manager, Pan-African Housing Group, Addis Ababa, Ethiopia

MRS. RUTH HABWE, Civic Leader, Nairobi, Kenya

MR. S. B. JONES, Executive Director, Manpower Division, Ministry of Finance and Economic Planning, Accra, Ghana

DR. NGUETE KIKHELA, Director General, Office National de la Recherche et du Developpment, Kinshasa, Zaire

DR. G. M. K. KPEDEKPO, Institute of Statistics and Applied Economics, Makerere University, Kampala, Uganda (Citizen of Ghana)

MRS. EDITH MADENGE, Public Health Officer, Ministry of Health; All African Women Conference, East/South Region, Dar-es-Salaam, Tanzania

MR. ZACHARIAH MALECHE, Department of Urban and Rural Physical Planning, Ministry of Lands and Settlement, Nairobi, Kenya

MR. ISMAIL MWISHASHI, Prime Minister's Office, Dar-es-Salaam, Tanzania

MR. GILBERT NJAU, Chief Planner, City Council of Nairobi, Nairobi, Kenya

MRS. FLORA NWAKUCHE, Commissioner, Ministry of Lands, Survey and Urban Development, Enugu, East Central State, Nigeria

MR. JERRY W. OWUOR, Senior Deputy Secretary, Ministry of Health, Nairobi, Kenya

MR. ADOLPHUS PATERSON, Journalist, Accra, Ghana

MR. MEBRAHTU YOHANNES, Bureau of Social Welfare, Ministry of Community Development and Social Affairs, Addis Ababa, Ethiopia

REPRESENTATIVES OF COSPONSORING ORGANIZATIONS

DR. J. MUGO GACHUHI, Institute for Development Studies, University of Nairobi, Nairobi, Kenya; *Seminar Coordinator*

DR. W. PARKER MAULDIN, Vice President, The Population Council, New York, New York, U.S.A.; Member, NAS–NRC International Steering Committee

DR. CHUKUKA OKONJO, Head, Department of Economics, and Dean, Faculty of the Social Sciences, University of Nigeria, Nsukka, Nigeria; Member, NAS–NRC International Steering Committee; *Seminar Cochairman*

MRS. PUSHPA NAND SCHWARTZ, NAS–NRC, Washington, D.C., U.S.A.; *Project Coordinator*

DR. GEORGE STOLNITZ, Department of Economics, Indiana University, Bloomington, Indiana, U.S.A.; Member, NAS–NRC International Steering Committee; *Seminar Cochairman*

MR. W. MURRAY TODD, NAS–NRC, Washington, D.C., U.S.A.; *Project Director*

DISCUSSANT

DR. JOHN C. CALDWELL, Demography Department, Australian National University, Canberra, A.C.T., Australia

Southeast Asia Seminar on Population Policy

VI

Manila, Philippines, 27 November–1 December 1973
Organization of Demographic Associates (Philippines)
Pacific Science Association, Hawaii (U.S.A.)
National Academy of Sciences–National Research Council (U.S.A.)

Twenty participants and discussants in the Southeast Asia seminar came from Indonesia, the Republic of Korea, Malaysia, the Philippines, Singapore, and Thailand. Participation from Korea, a country geographically outside the region, was arranged because of the relevance of Korean experience in population policy to the subject of the seminar.

Most national governments in the region have taken some measures in the last decade that can be said to constitute a fertility policy, but they are not pursuing and implementing these policy measures with equal vigor. All have spent large sums in the last 20 years on improving health facilities and starting public health programs that have resulted in a significant reduction in death rates. As a consequence, most countries have high population growth rates (Table 6).

Migration from the countryside to towns and cities is causing increasing concern to the governments in this region; to influence or adjust to such movements, a variety of policies, including increased investment in rural areas, have been implemented experimentally.

PERCEPTIONS OF POPULATION PROBLEMS

Population growth rates are regarded as a major problem in much of Southeast Asia because they handicap the countries in attaining their

73

TABLE 6 Five Southeast Asian Countries and Korea: Recent Population Data

Country	Estimated Population, Mid-1960 (millions)	Estimated Population, 1-1-73 (millions)	Births per 1,000 Population, 1972	Deaths per 1,000 Population, 1972	Annual Natural Increase, 1972 (%)	Years To Double Population	Population under Age 15 (%)	Life Expectancy at Birth, 1972 (years)	Urban Population (%)		Inhabitants per km², 1971	GNP per Capita at 1971 Market Prices (U.S. $)	Literate Population[a] (%)	Population per Physician (thousands)
									1970	1985 Projected				
Indonesia	93.51	128.12	45	18	2.7	26	45	48	17	22	85	80	60	21 (1972)
Republic of Korea	24.69	33.44	29	9	2.0	35	42	64	38	54	324	290	89	2 (1971)
Malaysia	8.11	11.68	38	10	2.8	25	44	60	45[b]	62[b]	37	400	69[b]	4 (1970)[b]
Philippines	27.41	41.29	43	11	3.2	22	43	59	34	41	127	240	72	2.8 (1970)
Singapore	1.63	2.20	23	5	1.8	39	38	70	100	100	3,675	1,200	75	0.7 (1971)
Thailand	26.39	39.08	41	11	3.0	23	46	62	15	19	69	210	68	11 (1970)

[a]Various years, 1965–1973.
[b]West Malaysia.
SOURCES: See Table 2, p. 8.

74

economic targets. The disadvantageous age distribution, with more than 40 percent of the people aged 15 or younger, is economically crippling in that it increases the demands on government budgets for education, health, and other services, as well as increased expenditures on subsistence. These demands drastically reduce the resources available for capital formation. Furthermore, population: resource ratios tend to deteriorate as population increases. Finally, concern is emerging for the environmental consequences of population growth. A Philippine participant described the serious situation in his country resulting from poor land management, soil erosion, and increased damage from floods.

Population distribution is a major policy concern in Malaysia, Indonesia, and the Philippines, all of which are attempting to attack the problem of rural-to-urban migration through direct governmental policy backed by private initiative and investment. The problems of correcting ethnic imbalances (especially in Malaysia), uneven sex distribution between urban and rural areas, and uneven opportunities and services in different sections of a country worry almost all governments of Southeast Asia.

International migration is viewed as a special problem for Singapore and, to a lesser extent, for Malaysia and Thailand. Poorly guarded border regions and tribal areas in Thailand are viewed as potential trouble spots, about which, it was noted, there is insufficient demographic information. The political consequences of international migration policies on neighboring countries are difficult to gauge, a point made in reference to the effect of Singapore's policies on its neighbors.

SOCIOCULTURAL ASPECTS

Policymakers in the region were criticized for generally ignoring the social and cultural aspects of people's lives when devising public policies. The design and execution of population policies sometimes blindly follow foreign models and methods, taking little account of local conditions and peculiarities.

A special difficulty in gaining wider acceptance of certain family-planning methods is that privacy, taken for granted in the West, is not possible for most married couples in the region.

To promote needed changes in laws and social customs, one participant said, it is critical that traditional elements in society be convinced and won over at an early stage. The political battle over reforms proposed in the Draft Marriage Law in Indonesia was cited as a case in point. Religious leaders launched a vigorous campaign against the law, which, among other measures, had sought to raise the minimum age for marriage, permit divorce, and legalize adoption. Their opposition resulted in a compromise that fell short of what many felt was very much needed to improve the status of women.

Another perspective on this subject is that social change reflects a clash between old and new values and is manifested in the differing attitudes of pressure groups operating in the political arena. Participants agreed that although care should be exercised in changing traditional attitudes, some traditional ways of life are not worth preserving. For example, the corruption that pervades some political systems must be changed even if it is at present culturally acceptable.

In designing programs and communicating them to the public, more efforts should be made to use traditional channels to reach the people; the use of shadow plays in Indonesia to promote family planning is an example of a skillful combination of old ways of communication with a new message. Western animated films are not effective in delivering the message on fertility regulation. People, it was suggested, do not take Mickey Mouse seriously. Traditional literature and folklore are full of morals and messages on family size; some advocate large families and some small. Those who design motivational strategies to promote family planning would do well to discover traditional lore advocating the small family and use it to increase the effectiveness of their messages.

URBANIZATION AND MIGRATION

Urbanization and migration were important topics in the seminar. Discussion ranged from an examination of why urban growth is so rapid to how investment can be spread to attain balanced urban growth outside the one or two large cities in each country. Can urbanization policy be used to improve the standard of living of the have-nots? How can the migrant be educated to adapt quickly to urban life? Is controlled urbanization a desirable and feasible policy goal?

One participant said that excessive rural–urban migration and urbanization should be seen as problems that show up "at the end of the line." To tackle them one must examine the basic problems affecting rural life, the villages, and the major sector of the economy— agriculture. One must find the reasons that induce villagers to move to cities.

The educational system was said to be partly responsible for the large-scale migration in the region. Practical skills of rural people are not improved by the prevailing educational curricula, and the schools do not instruct people to apply education to farm work. If anything, education now makes people less suited to rural life.

In the Philippines a regionalization program is decentralizing development planning, as well as administrative and investment decision making, into 11 geographical regions. Regional planning councils will draw up regional development programs coordinated by the central administration. A major objective of the decentralization program is to encourage local leaders to make decisions and formulate policies suited to the resource endowment and other conditions in each area so that both economic autonomy and interdependence are fostered, each depending on economies of scale in particular sectors. Furthermore, one city in each region will become the center for industrial and economic growth, the administration of government, and the provision of social services in the region. It is hoped that the program will decrease pressures for migration to Manila, now the largest urban center.

Some countries in the region have policies to promote new urban development outside the major city. Migration statistics cited for Malaysia show that rural-to-urban migration decreased substantially in the last census period. To improve the economic well-being of Malays, who are the ethnic majority, the government of Malaysia is actively encouraging them to settle in new urban centers. The object is to equalize income distribution among the different ethnic groups. Geographically, the policy is applied primarily in West Malaysia, where new towns of 60,000–70,000 are planned. Some think that the resulting better living conditions, urban infrastructure, and expanding opportunities may actually increase fertility among the Malay immigrants.

Migration in Indonesia has led to extremely rapid growth of the four largest cities but almost no growth of many others, especially in Java. The result, at least in the case of Jakarta, has been environmental deterioration and a fear of increasing social and economic disruption. The unemployment rate is said to be higher in Jakarta than in rural areas.

In Java the small size of many farms makes them uneconomical and encourages the drift of the underemployed or unemployed to urban centers. The government has attempted to settle the excess population of Java in Sumatra and some other islands, but this policy, called *transmigration*, has met with very limited success.

Indonesian participants said that Jakarta has recently instituted very strict rules about who may settle and work there, but this negative ap-

proach has seldom, if ever, been successful elsewhere. The real challenge
is how to make transmigration more attractive. One participant suggested that transmigration policies had failed because investment opportunities and infrastructure were not adequately provided in the
areas opened for settlement. A new approach to make business investment opportunities more attractive and to build a greater sense of
community participation among immigrants is essential to the success
of this policy.

The difficulty of attracting people away from existing large urban
centers and areas of high population density to smaller towns, rural
areas, or new settlements was said to exist also in Thailand and the
Philippines. Students and faculty prefer to attend the largest and best-
known universities or colleges in the big cities. Similarly, doctors and
other professionals are not easily persuaded to locate outside large
metropolitan areas.

STATUS OF WOMEN

Participants agreed that improving opportunities in education and
employment for women is a desirable objective in itself and would
motivate women to postpone marriage and have fewer children. But
effects on fertility depend on the kinds of employment women have
access to and the levels of education they reach: Unskilled farm employment and education below the tenth grade, according to a Thai
study, have no correlation with reduced fertility. No solution was
reached on the difficulty of expanding employment for women where
men are unemployed or underemployed.

Singapore and Korea do have high rates of female participation in the
labor force, along with relatively low and declining fertility rates. The
government of Singapore is trying to increase employment among
married women to decrease the need for imported labor. Korea in
recent years, it was said, has experienced a faster growth in female than
in male employment. Increased exposure to new ideas that labor force
participation gives women affects fertility in various ways. For example, the younger generation in Korea is now far more neutral in its
preference as to the sex of newborn children than were earlier generations. Improvement in the legal status of women also had an influence
on fertility. The law of inheritance in Korea was changed as a result of
strong pressure from women's organizations; there is now no
discrimination against female inheritance.

Attempts to improve the position of women by changing laws governing marriage, divorce, and inheritance have been made in Singapore, Indonesia, Thailand, and Malaysia. Women's organizations in Indonesia have been working actively to make traditional Moslem divorce laws less discriminatory against women. It was pointed out that changing a law, such as that setting the age of marriage, is far easier than enforcing it, as experience in Thailand has shown. In Singapore, however, a strict new divorce law is well enforced, resulting in a noticeable drop in the number of polygamous marriages.

Another issue of women's welfare is abortion. It is legal only in Singapore and Korea, and participants predicted it is not likely to be legalized in Malaysia, Indonesia, or the Philippines because of religious opposition. Student opinion and recent surveys conducted among women by the University of Indonesia, however, indicated an attitude favorable to legalized abortion. In Thailand, too, there seems to be less opposition to legalized abortion than was previously believed, but even now the preconditions for changing the law may not exist.

FOREIGN AID

Recognizing the contribution of foreign aid and technical advice, seminar participants were still highly critical of some aspects of foreign involvement in their countries. They pointed out that annual reviews and pressures surrounding aid allocation lead to artificial targets whose main result often is questionable statistical practices or, worse still, a resort to crude methods of achieving goals. Foreign consultants and counterparts, it was said, often end up experimenting with their pet solutions in political and cultural settings about which they have little understanding or knowledge.

In discussing research, more than one participant said that many worthwhile and badly needed studies are not undertaken because local funds are not available; research projects and priorities are too often decided by the availability of foreign funds.

On the positive side, it was said that invoking the authority of foreign study missions and advisers is often a useful technique for bureaucrats and scholars trying to convince political leaders that certain policy changes are necessary. The effectiveness of this technique depends, however, on whether the foreign group represents bilateral or multilateral assistance; the latter is much more useful for this purpose. One of the most valuable contributions of foreign assistance, it was agreed, is the transmission of other countries' experiences in population and development.

CONSTITUENCIES FOR POPULATION POLICY

The consensus of the group was that there are no political constituencies for fertility control as such in their countries. On the other hand, in all countries pressures exist, some insistent and powerful, for lowering morbidity and mortality. This finds expression in demands for better health facilities and public health programs. There are also demands for more public housing, transportation, slum clearance, and so on. There are political constituencies, primarily women's groups, that seek changes in marriage, divorce, and inheritance laws; the resulting public policies do affect fertility indirectly.

University students were identified as a key group that takes active stands on policy issues. One participant said that many Indonesian students are regularly engaged in voicing their opinions on government policy. Given their influence on shaping policies, student attitudes on fertility policy could be of great importance.

The apparent absence of constituencies for fertility control, it was suggested, may be due to inadequate information on the effects of population programs. For example, in Thailand it was reported that the military thought family planning would mean a lower total population (rather than a slower growth rate) in the future, which would hinder national defense. In spite of apparent resistance to family planning for Thailand as a whole, however, military hospitals initiated family-planning services for army personnel and their families because of the economic pressures on young military personnel with large families. In some countries many people opposed the use of intrauterine devices out of fear that they induce cancer. Participants agreed that such misunderstandings must be cleared up through publication of data and adequate public education before support can be gained for fertility-limiting policies.

MAKING POLICY WORK

Participants saw policymaking as the interplay of competing interests and needs that are balanced through the political process. Participants argued that local pressure groups should become more involved in policymaking. Technocrats in central government planning bureaus, it was said, tend to live in ivory towers. They must have access to a monitoring system that senses community demands; otherwise, they are like doctors attempting a diagnosis without seeing the patient. Leaders of pressure groups and local politicans are key people who have to be heard because they are in touch with the reality of community needs. Women's groups, religious leaders, and students were specially mentioned in references to Indonesia, Malaysia, and the Philippines as groups whose involvement, if not agreement, are crucial to successful policy implementation.

It was also argued that more must be learned about the life-style of the people at whom policy is directed and whose lives the government is attempting to change. For this purpose, more local social and anthropological research is needed.

Forecasting and projections for planning and policy were considered important by some participants. Others cautioned against putting much faith in figures derived from quick data-gathering exercises; they considered it dangerous to base precise targets and program objectives on such statistics. One participant went so far as to state that manpower planning is just another Western export, and, given the labor-supply situation in Southeast Asia, it is useless. Another said that six different studies in Malaysia on manpower planning had produced six contradictory strategies, because each was based on a different concept of the kind of Malaysian society expected in the future.

This line of reasoning was echoed in arguments that little is really known about what population policies will work and with what results. In reality, policies are made piecemeal to deal with crises or to correct deteriorating situations; it is just not possible to wait for adequate data and research.

A participant noted the unanticipated consequences of policy, citing an example from his country where mechanization of agriculture reduced the need for farm labor, but did not result in reduced fertility and family size. Farmers now want more children who can migrate to cities to earn money to send back for the purchase and upkeep of the new machinery! This outcome suggests that the expected effect on fertility of reduced need for farm labor was offset by the need for cash-earning capacity.

An integrated approach to population policy is needed, one that incorporates family planning and health, education, and other social and welfare policies and, in turn, forms an integral part of development planning. In Singapore, a small city–state with limited land area, public policy is made quickly and executed vigorously; the leadership feels it cannot afford to let the country be overtaken by events. Even a slight shift in demographic trends, such as a small increase in the fertility rate, could have a large effect on Singapore's economic welfare. The worry is that even the existing structure of Singapore's population will make difficult demands on the economy and on policymakers. Housing, taxation, immigration, labor, and employment policies are carefully synchronized to keep the influence of demographic changes within manageable limits. The national leadership is committed to improving the quality of life of its citizens and to upgrading the skills and quality of its population. Although Singapore is considered a very special case, the success of its policies in influencing people's lives and cultural habits is a powerful example for the region.

In the Philippines, a Commission on Population has been created to serve as the coordinating body to oversee the implementation of population projects and policies executed by public and private agencies. To date, the emphasis has been on clinical family-planning services, training, and information. At first the commission concentrated on reducing fertility through family planning, but now it is beginning to emphasize population education in all schools and to support population-related social and economic research. Commission officials believe that so far they have tackled the obvious and attained some easy early successes, but now the commission is seeking to broaden its scope.

To help chart a broader course on population policy, the Philippine government is soon expected to undertake a national study on Population, Resources, Environment, and the Philippine Future.

A program to prepare an inventory of policies with population implications and to market appropriate policy proposals to each of the various ministries concerned was suggested by a participant. The Revised Administrative Code and the Reorganization Plan, both concerned with overhauling the executive branch of the government, will be examined for possible population implications and for areas in which population policies could be developed. Industrial policy was also identified as an example of a key area that had been overlooked from the population perspective.

POLICY OPTIONS

Among the several policy options for the future, financial incentives and disincentives affecting fertility stimulated a good deal of interest.

Some governments in the region are already moving in this direction, using tax exemption measures, family and housing allowances, and the like. There was strong feeling that these new policies should be carefully studied to see that their impact does not fall mainly on the poorer segments of society while favoring higher income groups. On the other hand, it was observed, many of the poor would not be affected at all by disincentives because their incomes are below the taxable threshold.

Promoting old-age assistance through improved social security was considered a desirable option; limited financial resources and lack of administrative machinery for implementation were cited as the major constraints.

Family-planning services, including the provision of an adequate choice of contraceptives, participants agreed, should remain an important part of all national programs. Special attention, however, should also be given to education and motivation. Some added that family-planning services should be available to everyone, including the unmarried.

In response to an observation that the rising cost of children to the family had resulted, historically, in a drop in fertility, some participants doubted that the same mechanism would work in their region. Because children are still immensely important in the people's value-orientation, there are limits to what disincentives can achieve. In some countries, after an initial drop in response to policy measures—incentives, disincentives, and family-planning services—fertility seems to have stabilized on a plateau that is still higher than desirable.

A small number felt that it is time that governments take bold and aggressive policy steps, such as changing family allowances and housing policies in an antinatalist direction. A program involving only government employees at first could serve as an example and invitation to business enterprises and labor organizations to cooperate in such experiments.

This seminar demonstrated that the differences among regions of the developing world are reflected strongly in the sentiments of the seminar participants. The social justification for fertility reduction and for the deliberate modification of distribution of people has already been established. Whether current policies and programs are effective was a matter of considerable debate.

PARTICIPANTS

MR. HI SUP CHUNG, The Korean Institute for Social Development, Seoul, Korea

MR. BENJAMIN D. DE LEON, Deputy Executive Director, Commission on Population, Makati, Rizal, Philippines

MR. ARMAND V. FABELLA, Chairman, Reorganization Commission, Manila, Philippines

MR. MOHAMMED ANWAR FAZAL, Director, Promotion and Investment, Penang Development Corporation, Penang, Malaysia

DR. F. LANDA JOCANO, Chairman, Department of Anthropology, University of the Philippines, Diliman, Quezon City, Philippines

DR. CONRADO Ll. LORENZO, JR., Executive Director, Commission on Population, Makati, Rizal, Philippines

MR. JUAN L. MERCADO, Press Foundation of Asia, Manila, Philippines

DR. YETTY RIZALI NOOR, Delegate to the U.N. Commission on the Status of Women, Jakarta, Indonesia

DR. PANG ENG FONG, Director, Economic Research Centre, University of Singapore, Singapore

MR. VICENTE B. PAQUEO, School of Economics, University of the Philippines, Diliman, Quezon City, Philippines

DR. VISID PRACHUABMOH, Director, The Institute of Population Studies, Chulalongkorn University, Bangkok, Thailand

MISS JAWALAKSANA RACHAPAETAYAKOM, Senior Demographer, Manpower Planning Division, National Economic and Social Development Board, Bangkok, Thailand

DR. HAMZAH SENDUT, Vice Chancellor, Universiti Sains Malaysia, Penang, Malaysia

MR. KUSUMOSUWIDHO SISDJIATMO, Research Staff, Demographic Institute, Department of Economics, University of Indonesia, Jakarta, Indonesia

MR. WIROSARDJONO SOETJIPTO, Executive Secretary, Inter Indonesian Municipality Organization, Jakarta, Indonesia

DR. KOWIT VORAPIPATANA, Chief, Adult Education Division, Ministry of Education, Bangkok, Thailand

MRS. ANN WEE, Head, Department of Social Work, University of Singapore, Singapore

OBSERVERS AND DISCUSSANTS

MRS. KATJA BOH, Senior Researcher, Institute of Sociology, University of Ljubljana, Ljubljana, Yugoslavia

MR. J. ARISTEO G. GONZALEZ, Brotherhood of Asian Trade Unionists, Manila, Philippines

DR. GAVIN W. JONES, The Population Council, Jakarta, Indonesia

MR. JAMES PHILLIPS, Field Associate, The Population Council; Population Institute, University of the Philippines, Manila, Philippines

REPRESENTATIVES OF COSPONSORING ORGANIZATIONS

DR. JOHN E. BARDACH, Director, Hawaii Institute of Marine Biology, University of Hawaii at Manoa, Kanoehe, Hawaii, U.S.A. (Representative, Pacific Science Association)

DR. MERCEDES CONCEPCION, Dean, Population Institute, University of the Philippines; President, Organization of Demographic Associates, Manila, Philippines; *Seminar Cochairman*

DR. PAUL DEMENY, Vice President, The Population Council, New York, New York, U.S.A.; Member, NAS–NRC International Steering Committee; *Seminar Cochairman*

DR. BETTY P. MATHEWS, Professor of Health Education, University of Washington, Seattle, Washington, U.S.A.; Member, NAS–NRC International Steering Committee

DR. ASOK MITRA, Secretary to the President of India, Rashtrapati Bhavan, New Delhi, India; Member, NAS–NRC International Steering Committee

DR. PAVAO NOVOSEL, Faculty of Political Science, University of Zagreb, Zagreb, Yugoslavia; Member, NAS–NRC International Steering Committee

MRS. PUSHPA NAND SCHWARTZ, NAS–NRC, Washington, D.C., U.S.A.; *Project Coordinator*

MR. W. MURRAY TODD, NAS–NRC, Washington, D.C., U.S.A.; *Project Director*

DR. MYRON WEINER, Department of Political Science, Massachusetts Institute of Technology, Cambridge, Massachusetts, U.S.A.; Chairman NAS–NRC International Steering Committee

Summary
and Committee
Reflections

VII

WHAT IS POPULATION POLICY?

At the beginning of the series of seminars described in this report the steering committee asked, "What is population policy?" As a point of departure, we took the United Nations' definition of population policy:

> ... measures and programmes designed to contribute to the achievement of economic, social, demographic, political and other collective goals through affecting critical demographic variables, namely the size and growth of the population, its geographic distribution (national and international) and its demographic characteristics. . . .*

We agreed that the definition should be expanded to include measures and programs that *are likely* to affect critical demographic variables as well as those *designed* to do so. We also distinguished between policies that *influence* population variables and those that are *responsive* to population changes. An example of a *population-influencing* policy is the decision to provide innoculation against measles, a potentially lethal disease. The result of the policy is to decrease child mortality. An example of a *population-responsive* policy is building schools where people are, or building enough schools for all the children of a certain

*United Nations Economic and Social Council, Population Commission. *Report of the* ad hoc *Consultative Group of Experts on Population Policy* (E/CN.9/267), 23 May 1972, p. 6.

86

age in a given area. The number of classrooms built is dictated by the number of children; it is a response to a population variable. The definition of population policy thus needs to include the ways governments respond to population change.

Policies may influence population variables directly or indirectly. Family-planning services and legal abortion, for example, can have a direct effect on population size by reducing the number of births. Decreasing tax exemptions or reducing family allowances for dependents may indirectly reduce the number of births by influencing parental decisions on family size. These policies can be made at different levels of government decision making (national, regional, state, or local) and by different organs of a government, depending on its constitutional form or system.

When governments influence the way people begin life (fertility), how they end it (mortality), and where they live (spatial distribution), they explicitly or implicitly have population-influencing policies.

HOW SOME DEVELOPING COUNTRIES VIEW POPULATION GROWTH

Studies of population in the West anticipate a world population approaching 7 billion by the end of this century and conclude that this doubling since the mid-1960s is bound to present the global community with extraordinary stresses, some of which can be predicted and many of which can only be imagined. The pervasiveness of this global view in Western literature contrasts with the diverse opinions held by seminar participants from developing regions, who saw population issues essentially from national standpoints.

Anyone accustomed to the conventional there-is-a-population-explosion approach would be impressed with the diversity of ways in which seminar participants perceived population growth and change. Perceptions naturally are filtered through cultural and normative lenses. It may seem banal to say that political, economic, class, ideological, religious, and other influences affect people's perceptions, just as they do their knowledge of the "facts" (and what the facts are in many developing countries may not be easy to discover), but it is important to keep this observation in mind.

Population growth was regarded by some as desirable because of low settlement densities in certain regions, because of the need for people where there are believed to be extensive exploitable natural resources, where the current population is insufficient to provide a large domestic market, where large numbers are thought necessary for defense, or where population growth is regarded as desirable simply for social and economic change.

The majority, however, found population growth a serious problem for their countries because it dilutes the advances in development that can be and have been achieved. There is not enough time or resources to catch up with the growing needs for health care, school buildings and school teachers, and new jobs for the many people entering the work force. The effects of a large number of children, usually un-planned, on the welfare of the family, the health of the mother, and the development of the children were cited as some of the negative aspects of too rapid growth from the "micro" or familial viewpoint.

One element of growth that bothered virtually all the seminar partici-pants was the uncontrolled expansion of urban centers.

Perceptions of population problems not only vary from one country to another but vary within countries and even within governments. A minister of health is likely to see infant mortality as the key issue. The head of a municipality and an urban planner may be concerned with the high rate of migration. A minister of defense may give priority to increasing manpower for his army. A development planner may be pre-occupied with employment for young people entering the labor force.

The seminar participants reported these various perspectives along with their own experiences and occupations as journalists, social workers, and civic leaders, as well as policymakers.

Global population problems in terms of sheer numbers and the con-tinued growth of world population in relation to global resources were given less importance by the seminar participants from developing countries than a wide range of other problems far closer to their own national and personal experiences. Specifically, they cited the follow-ing problems:

Reducing Mortality and Morbidity

Premature death and the prevalence of disease are still major factors in the population calculus of people in the developing world. It is gen-erally accepted that the worldwide decline in mortality, particularly of the young, has precipitated the present rapid growth of population. Im-proved public and private sanitation, public health care, and some improvement in nutrition have resulted in a sharp decline in death rates in almost all developing countries. Previously high birth rates have remained about the same, and the result is a sharp increase in the number of surviving children.

However, what is perhaps less widely recognized is that this decline in disease and death rates has not been uniform over the developing world. Some countries still have high death rates; others with declining death rates have uneven patterns of decline by ethnic group, economic class, region, and so on. In some cases infant mortality in developing countries is 10 times that of developed countries. And in such situations the reduction of mortality takes priority over virtually all other issues. Debilitating diseases are also a major cause for concern in all developing countries. In some the effects of debilitating disease are only now beginning to be estimated, but the level of productivity of those who suffer and the total output of the economy are surely reduced. Finally, the human and economic toll of sporadic epidemics and malnutrition is incalculable.

Strains of Urban Growth

In many countries of the developing world there is a single major city, usually the capital, in which urban growth is taking place at an unprecedented rate and where up to 15 percent or more of the country's total population lives. In other countries the rate of movement from rural areas to urban centers, and the rate of movement from smaller to larger urban centers, causes serious concern.

Most participants expressed the view that rapid migration to cities is undesirable because it produces social and economic problems that defy solution, given the resources available in most developing countries. One school of thought extolled the virtues of rural as opposed to urban life because it equated migration with a vast array of problems: Too rapid urbanization strains health, education, police, water, sanitation, and other municipal services and generates a vast pool of unemployed or underemployed. Squatter settlements on the fringes of cities were generally deplored. They were said to invade public or private land, to breed delinquency, political activism, disease and epidemics. Yet, it was acknowledged that their inhabitants are probably better off than in the rural environments from where they came.

A countervailing argument was that the only way to move into the modern world is to industrialize, and industrialization requires an urban society. But only a few participants favored urbanization as the most suitable course to pursue. Most sought to discourage migration by creating or enhancing rural amenities, employment, and investment opportunities.

The imbalance between the services provided rural and urban communities was addressed in each seminar. There was an underlying skepticism as to whether planners and officials who live in cities can submerge their interests in favor of accelerated rural-development programs.

Expanding Social Services

High rates of population growth make it exceedingly difficult to achieve targets in education, health, and governmental services. Many social and welfare problems associated with rapid population growth stem from the difficulty of financing the services, on the one hand, and from training and employing skilled people to provide the services, on the other.

Rights and Welfare of Women and Children

Women's rights to education and employment and emancipation from the domination of husbands, fathers, and other male members of society found expression in the context of family life and welfare. Awareness appears to be growing (with great differences from region to region) of the need for women to take a larger part in family decisions. How many children a couple will have and how closely spaced they will be are emerging as decisions for both husband and wife—a new development in most traditional societies.

A lesser, but comparable, concern was voiced with respect to the welfare of children, their need for adequate nutrition, education, eventual employment opportunities, and family rights.

Employment and Unemployment

Rapid population growth has led to large pools of unemployed and underemployed in many developing countries, and there is no prospect of reducing or stabilizing the labor force in the foreseeable future. This was regarded as a major population problem in all the seminars, particularly in South and Southeast Asia. Augmenting these pools with women who want to work and have the educational qualifications to do so does not comfort the manpower planner or development minister.

Differences among ethnic groups in employment in, and management of, certain sectors of the economy have produced tensions in Africa and some parts of Asia. These are likely to increase as the pressure for jobs intensifies with the growing numbers of young people entering the labor market. Visible disparities of economic power aggravate the discontent.

The political implications of unemployment for governments in power were mentioned in each seminar. The need to provide employment for both educated and uneducated is seen as an immediate problem for almost all countries represented in the seminars, and it has already reached a critical state in some countries.

Committee Comment

The seminars took place in 1973 before the participants (or we) were aware of the current state of world supplies of food and fuel. Mention was made only of food shortages in Bangladesh and the Sahelian zone in Africa. We suspect that if the seminars were held in 1974, the shortages (both existing and projected) of food and the effects of increased petroleum prices on transport, utilities, and fertilizer production, as well as on balance of payments, would be issues of profound concern.

The effects of rapid population growth on the environment, a recent preoccupation in developed countries, was discussed briefly at each seminar, but is not an issue of great concern in most developing countries. Environmental problems of water supply and disposal of human wastes have long had serious consequences for health and even survival in many countries, but these are generally thought of as problems of poverty rather than of population.

POPULATION POLICIES

The observation of some participants that population policy is a developed-country concept is perhaps attributable to the common practice of equating population policy with family planning. It is true that the great recent impetus to fertility reduction in high-fertility areas originated in the developed countries and has not been accompanied by equally visible calls for lowering mortality or comprehensive planning for the optimum distribution of people. The issue, however, is not the origin of the concern for population policy but whether it is germane to current needs.

A wide spectrum of policies to influence population was described by seminar participants. The committee has divided such policies into six categories:

- Policies that influence mortality and morbidity;
- Policies that influence fertility directly;
- Policies that influence fertility indirectly;
- Policies related to composition;
- Policies related to distribution (including urbanization); and
- Policies that influence international migration.

Mortality and Morbidity

In all societies, for obvious humanitarian reasons, policies to reduce morbidity and mortality have the highest priority. Indeed, the African seminar identified the reduction of mortality and morbidity as the most important area for comprehensive government policymaking, undoubtedly because this region has the highest mortality in the world.

Lowering mortality and morbidity was believed to be indispensable to fertility reduction everywhere, although no quantitative relationships or thresholds were identified.

Many participants argued that more government attention should be given to relieving the shortage of medical and paramedical personnel and increasing health, nutritional, and related services for rural populations. As city dwellers and members of higher socioeconomic groups, the participants were uncomfortably sensitive to the vast difference between health services provided even the very poor in cities and those provided rural people. The costs of extending service to rural areas loom large, but it was agreed that these costs must be borne somehow and policies effected to eliminate urban–rural inequities.

Policies That Influence Fertility Directly

Population policies to influence fertility in developing countries are of fairly recent origin. A few governments in such countries have official pronatalist views, more governments support family planning for maternal and child health and other humanitarian reasons, and a growing number of governments have been adopting antinatalist policies.

Among the countries represented at the seminars, most in South and Southeast Asia support family-planning efforts. In the Middle East some countries have antinatalist policies, while others support family planning for maternal and child health reasons. One, Kuwait, has a pronatalist policy. Similarly, many islands in the Caribbean have adopted antinatalist policies, whereas in Central and Latin America only Costa Rica, Colombia, and Mexico have such policies. Most Central American countries and several South American countries provide or permit some support to family-planning programs for maternal and child health reasons. In sub-Sahara Africa support for such programs is quite restricted. Ghana and Kenya are the principal countries with official antinatalist policies, and a few countries support family planning for nondemographic reasons.

In the South and Southeast Asia seminars it was agreed that family-planning services should be provided free or at a low price by the state, or through state-sponsored schemes, to all who want them. A range of such services should be offered, so that individual differences in attitudes about the acceptability of different methods can be accommodated. Full information should be provided on the variety of methods, their safety, convenience, cost, side effects, and effectiveness, as well as where services may be obtained.

This policy approach was generally approved by participants in the Middle East seminar. It was partially accepted by Latin American participants in the Commonwealth Caribbean–Latin America seminar, on condition that the justification for such services is based on maternal and child health and other humanitarian reasons, not demographic objectives. Commonwealth Caribbean participants did not have these reservations. African participants also thought family-planning services should be available to those who want them, but the majority rejected the idea that population policies to lower rates of population growth are needed.

In both the Commonwealth Caribbean–Latin America and the African seminars concern was expressed over the moral implications of freely available contraceptive supplies and "premature" education of young women in their use. The Middle East seminar raised the issue in terms of women's using fertility-limiting methods without their husbands' knowledge. In each discussion on ethical concerns partici-

pants worried that traditional decisions of the family may be influenced by the state without due regard to the effect on family life.

As noted earlier, government interest in changing fertility levels in
the developing countries is recent. Since programs designed to lower
fertility were almost nonexistent before 1960 and only a few countries
adopted such measures during the next 5 years, there has been little
time to implement existing programs or to assess their impact.

ABORTION

In all the seminars there was considerable discussion of induced abortion. Recent legalization of abortion in India, Iran, Tunisia, South
Korea, and Singapore was believed to be due to the desire of the governments to lower fertility. In Latin America, by contrast, much of the
impetus for providing family-planning services is thought to have
arisen because of the medical profession's concern with morbidity and
mortality resulting from illegal abortions performed by unskilled
persons under primitive, unsanitary conditions. Although abortion is
widespread in Latin America, nowhere has it been legalized, largely because of religious opposition.

There was considerable diversity of opinion about the desirability of
legalizing abortion. Some participants thought it desirable for demographic reasons, and many thought it desirable for maternal health or as
a human right. In general, the South and Southeast Asian seminars
supported liberalization of abortion laws, and opinion was split in the
Middle East and the African seminars.

INCENTIVES AND DISINCENTIVES

Although direct incentives and disincentives to reduce fertility are not
generally used in family-planning programs around the world, they
were discussed in the Asian and Middle East seminars. (African and
Latin American seminar participants expressed little interest in the
subject.) Ideas presented included raising the cost of having children by
reducing maternity leave and benefits, reducing family and children's
allowances, taxing to penalize births beyond a certain number, and
paying women to avoid conception for specific periods. Fertility
disincentives have been used extensively in Singapore and to some
extent in Tunisia. In India experimental incentive projects include a
deferred-bond scheme (akin to a retirement fund), which is being tested
among women workers in several tea estates. An experimental educa-

tional-bond scheme in Taiwan was mentioned. All these projects have been under trial only for a short time.

Participants expressed two reservations: whether disincentive programs will disproportionately hurt the poor, and whether incentive schemes are administratively and culturally feasible. Most people in poor countries are below taxable income levels, do not live in municipal housing, and do not receive family allowances. Hence, policy levers for using tax, housing, or welfare incentives appear to be weak. Even so, participants predicted that policymakers will give increasing attention to the possible use of incentives to lower fertility, especially payments to nonpregnant women. Possibly such incentives would have the additional political attraction of being income-redistribution measures, assuming that the poor socioeconomic strata respond positively to payment schemes.

STERILIZATION

Sterilization policies were hardly discussed in any of the seminars, even in the South Asian setting, where there has been considerable experimentation with this method of reducing fertility. An exception was the statement by a participant from the Commonwealth Caribbean area that young women who do not care to use conventional contraceptives and have had all the children they want are having difficulty persuading male physicians to sterilize them, even though it is legal.

Policies That Influence Fertility Indirectly

Throughout the seminars the belief was expressed that as development proceeds, so will the decline of mortality and, subsequently, the decline in fertility. Frequently, the question was posed, "If this is indeed the case, why is it not possible to wait for the inevitable as we continue with development?" Or, phrased another way, "There is no need to take steps to affect fertility directly; all our resources should be directed to accelerating development, not preventing births."

In the African seminar several participants stated their belief in the fertility-influencing effects of education and health measures. The salutary effects of social restructuring and income redistribution were mentioned by several Latin American participants.

Implicit in these arguments is the assumption that development could result in a sustained demographic transition before the consequences of rapid population growth overwhelmed resources. The South Asian, Southeast Asian, and Middle East participants did not make this assumption.

In all seminars there were long discussions of policy measures that might have the effect of reducing fertility indirectly, or that were considered necessary for the success of direct fertility-reducing schemes. The following measures, some of which were quite controversial, were suggested:

- A higher age of marriage;
- Equalization of inheritance laws for females;
- Elimination of polygamy;
- Acceptable and easy-to-achieve divorce;
- Provision of equal educational, political, and economic rights and opportunities for women;
- Laws restricting child labor;
- Compulsory elementary education;
- Family life and sex education;
- Equal inheritance and support rights for adopted and illegitimate children;
- Creation of youth service corps;
- Widespread availability of old-age retirement benefits; and
- Modernizing land-tenure systems.

These measures might or might not be instituted on their own merit as socially desirable, with a secondary effect of reducing fertility. Most of the discussions of these policies dealt with costs and benefits in political and social rather than economic terms, although the economic costs of old-age benefit schemes were generally thought to exceed the resources of most developing countries. In several of the suggested policy areas there would be little or no direct cost to the government.

In no case were the participants able to assess the quantitative effects on fertility of these indirect policies.

Composition of Population

In conventional demographic terms *composition* of population includes categories such as numbers of people at different age levels, ethnic distribution, and the ratio of men to women in various age brackets. For our purposes the meaning of composition includes also the usage of economists and sociologists: i.e., the quality of the population in terms of education, health, and characteristics of the labor force.

The need for policies to effect change in the composition of population arises from several considerations. There is an urgent need to reduce public welfare burdens and dependency ratios and to increase the proportion of people in nonagricultural employment. Developing countries need to raise labor force capabilities for more sophisticated technology, which requires improving education and skills. Most participants favored increasing the proportion of working women across the entire spectrum of occupations.

There was some consensus in all seminars that universal primary education, and particularly for females, would bring about significant and enduring change.

Distribution of Population

The policies that countries use to alter current or anticipated population distribution have been remarkably different. The questions that surround distribution, including urbanization and migration issues, are in some ways more complex than those of fertility and mortality, and distribution policies tend to be formulated separately from mortality and fertility policies.

Differences among distribution policies were found to stem in large part from the great diversity in size and character of national political units. The geographic scales of a country like Kuwait or the city–state of Singapore stand in sharp contrast to the vast expanses of Brazil or India. The encapsulated unity of a Caribbean island is totally different from the environmental diversity of Iran.

Planners, it was agreed, must decide simultaneously how to encourage urbanization as a concomitant to modernity and how to formulate policies to keep people in agricultural communities, either through inducements to stay or restrictions on their right to move.

The idea of preventing people from moving from rural areas was discussed in the African, South Asian, and Southeast Asian seminars, but strong opposition was voiced against any form of "pass control" that would require citizens to prove their right to be in some part of their country.

Participants reported widespread interest in locating industrial centers in rural environments as a way to expand the work horizons of

rural people and thereby to reduce their propensity to move to the
city. A related goal would be to create small urban centers in order to
distribute population more evenly in the available land and to reduce
pressure on the major city or cities. It was understood that "rural industrialization"—although the term was not fully defined—requires cooperation among entrepreneurs, central government, and local
authorities in complex ways, from the provision of capital and resources to the creation of networks of transportation, power, and
other state-supplied services.

In some places the concept of rural industrialization, or a modification of it, has resulted in attempts to " regionalize." The central government decrees the establishment of several regional centers and provides
a core of government services and jobs that then attract industry and
state-supported facilities such as schools, colleges, and ancillary activities.

A second approach seeks to establish satellite towns around or near
existing large cities. A third idea is to create an urbanized "spoke" extending from a major center, with the amenities of urban life provided
along the spoke. Because the spokes are long and narrow, public
transportation can be provided along linear central corridors, separated
by areas no wider than walking distance to the transportation line.
Industries and jobs can be located at the end of the spoke and in the
central city. This plan, in the "twin city" plan of Bombay, has been
supplemented by providing a housing scheme that can be self-financing
and an industrial land-development scheme that is also virtually self-
financing.

Another approach to problems of rural–urban distribution is the
upgrading of rural centers that have the potential to become urbanized.
The government agrees to provide villages with materials to build a
sanitary water supply if one is needed, materials for a clinic and a
school, and credit to hire a teacher and a nurse or paramedic. After
this, it is up to the villagers to exploit the proffered assistance. The
point of the scheme, aside from the development of community spirit
and self-reliance, is to enable the central authorities to plan the location
and distribution of many rural centers so that villagers have less need
to move to cities to find services.

Policies that affect agriculture also indirectly affect the distribution
of people. Mechanization of agriculture may drive some people off the
land, while conventional education of rural youth often makes them
want to move to the city. Building rural roads makes it easier to leave
for the city or to live in the city for a part of the week and back on the
farm for the other. The Green Revolution, with its necessary invest-

ments in fertilizer, special seeds, regular water supply, and pesticides, tends to drive some farmers who do not have access to these factors of production off the land and into the cities.

To relocate major administrative units outside the cities in new centers is difficult because civil servants (including university teachers, doctors, and other professionals) do not want to move from the urban amenities they now enjoy. The use of tax exemptions, credit, special salary incentives and, occasionally, disincentives (such as job dismissal for refusal to move) were suggested ways to make such policy work.

In a few places (Brazil is the most obvious) well-developed schemes are in effect to populate certain regions in order to exploit presently underutilized resources. Participants described the failure so far of a plan in Indonesia to move large numbers of people away from over-populated Java to less developed and thinly populated Sumatra.

Distribution policy is still in the experimental stages. Although all seminars found it an intriguing subject, it was not one that produced many concrete examples of successfully executed policies. Some interesting and potentially rewarding experimentation is taking place in the design of cities and in imaginative and humane approaches to housing for the poor, rural enhancement, urban renewal and reconstruction, and in developing whole new urban networks. But jurisdictional disputes, lack of experience or appropriate models, and a scarcity of experts present major obstacles to action.

International Migration

Although migration across international boundaries is extensive in the developing world, the seminars did not emphasize policies to control it. Three types of such migration were identified, each with different policy implications and responses: (1) movement of skilled and un-skilled manpower, (2) forced movement, and (3) seasonal migration.

The influx of skilled manpower is uniquely exemplified in Kuwait, where aliens account for over 50 percent of the total population and 70 percent of the labor force.

The temporary migration of North African, Yugoslav, and Turkish labor to West European factories, principally in France and Germany, and of Malaysian and Indonesian workers to Singapore, are examples of international flows of unskilled labor. Government policy in sender countries promotes the flow to relieve unemployment and to benefit from the repatriation of workers' earnings.

Policies to encourage outmigration of unskilled labor exist in some densely populated Caribbean island nations. As education becomes more available and the skills of the island people increase, however, the educated become the emigrants, seeking opportunity to use their training elsewhere.

The effects of several large war-related international movements were also noted. The Palestinian refugees are a dramatic example of how much such a movement may affect the demographic structure of a recipient country, in that over half the population of Jordan is said to be of Palestinian origin.

Policies to force migration also affect the demographic structure of the sending community, as in East Africa, where the expulsion of Asians has deprived the region of a substantial part of its commercial and professional classes and opened new opportunities for the Africans.

In many developing areas international migration of manpower is seasonal. In such cases host-government policies usually govern the level and rate of migration and place restrictions on employment opportunities. Implicit policies to send and receive on the part of the governments involved are also common.

Some countries have policies that restrict the outward flow of skilled personnel and make it difficult for educated manpower to emigrate. It was observed that such policies are effective only in countries with extremely rigid controls.

Countries with explicit policies affecting international migration tend to integrate migration with manpower and human-resources policies. Where there is high dependence on alien labor, governments seek to reduce this dependence either by planning for the local population's eventual takeover of alien-held jobs or by modifying the economic structure to reduce the need for imported labor. For example, the government of Singapore consciously discourages industries that need unskilled labor, since most such labor is alien.

The historical functions of international migration, to alleviate overpopulation or to colonize new territories, have long since been weakened by a much-reduced flow of people and by intricate political considerations that, although varying from one country to another, tend to be inhibitory.

POLICY FORMULATION AND ADMINISTRATION: ACTORS AND CONSTITUENCIES

Policy Formulation

In all seminars there was lively and sometimes contentious discussion of how population policies are made and who makes them. In general, the seminar participants agreed that population policies are formulated at the national level by small groups of people, often in planning agencies and health ministries, with little or no public debate or participation. The influence of external (foreign) agencies and institutions, particularly in matters relating to fertility, was said to be substantial and generated in two ways: through funds made available for fertility-limiting programs and through foreign training of the members of the planning group (in one country, called the "Berkeley Mafia"). Research on such questions as the incidence of abortion and attitude toward preferred family size by demographic research centers within a less-developed country is also a stimulant to new policies and programs.

According to the participants, none of the countries represented has any significant political parties actively pressing for the adoption of policies explicitly intended to affect demographic behavior. But constituencies do exist to which the government can turn for support. There is often considerable public involvement by religious institutions, women's organizations, and bar associations in such policy issues as proposed new marriage, divorce, inheritance, and adoption laws, even though these changes are usually advocated for social justice rather than for possible demographic objectives. Family-planning activities have often been initiated by medical associations, as well as by women's groups and local planned parenthood associations. Abortion laws also provoke considerable public involvement, again from religious bodies, women's organizations—typically small groups of middle- and upper-class women in a few urban centers—and the medical profession.

In several seminars discussion focused on the constraints on policy-makers, rather than on public demands for policies. Participants reported a catalog of constraints: the ideologies and outlook of the dominant political elite itself; the tendency of leftist groups to view population policies as a diversion from fundamental "structural" changes; the hostility of the right wing to policies affecting the traditional role of women; opposition to family-planning services, abortion legislation, and marriage-reform laws by some religious institutions; conflicting claims by ministries within the government over the allocation of limited government resources to health and family-planning services versus other much needed programs; and, finally, the skills, motivation, and integrity of the administrators themselves to effectively carry out programs that have been agreed upon.

Many seminar participants emphasized the role that may be played by strong, charismatic national leaders in minimizing these constraints. Endorsement of a population policy by such leaders reduces political opposition, makes a singular impression on the populace, and, most importantly, has an impact on the implementation of programs and on the allocation of resources for such programs. Examples were cited—in Iran, Tunisia, Singapore, Mexico, the Philippines—where the position taken by a national political leader made a policy difference.

Most seminars discussed how population policies could be defined— or redefined— to expand political constituencies that might initiate and support such policies. In several pronatal countries of sub-Sahara Africa and Latin America, participants reported, even when population-limitation policies and programs are rejected for ideological and political reasons, some of the same programs (e.g., family planning as part of maternal and child health programs) receive support because of their benefits to women and their families. Several participants, especially in the South and Southeast Asia seminars, noted that population policies could receive greater political support if, at the same time, they distribute income more equitably. Thus, there might be political support for social security programs, financial payments to women for not having children, expanded educational systems that provide greater opportunities for women, and a variety of incentive schemes that simultaneously discourage fertility and increase the income of the poor. Political support for income-distribution policies, it was noted, would be forthcoming in many countries regardless of their impact on fertility behavior.

A typical dilemma is that the policies (such as legalized abortion) most likely to influence the fertility behavior of a portion of the populace are often not politically feasible; whereas the policies that are most politically feasible (such as income-distribution policies) are those whose effect on fertility is least understood. Several participants argued for incentive schemes as programs that are both politically salable and likely to have fertility-dampening effects.

Policy and Program Implementation

A recurrent theme of the seminar was the ineffectiveness of many programs to influence fertility behavior. Some difficulties encountered

by family-planning programs appear to be typical of government programs in general: lack of skilled personnel; conflicts between agencies;
poor communication between central offices and the field; inadequate
financing; low morale and corruption. Added to these are problems
peculiar to family planning: the unwillingness of doctors to make
greater use of practitioners of traditional medicine and local midwives
as disseminators of family-planning materials and as paramedical as-
sistants; the problem of finding enough trained personnel to work in
rural areas; and the conflicting claims on resources between health and
family-planning programs.

Since the demand for family-planning services is low in some countries and few organized local groups are actively pressing for programs,
built-in means for correcting program deficiencies are inadequate.
Program effectiveness, particularly in family planning, is usually measured by "number of births prevented" or "number of acceptors"—
indices that do not provide much feedback to policymakers and administrators. Participants urged that voluntary associations, e.g.,
women's associations, be asked to play a more active role in the critical
evaluation of programs at the local level and in suggesting modifications.

The possibility of using youth corps and similar public-service-
oriented, short-term, trained people for some educational tasks in
family-planning, health, and nutrition programs received attention in the
Middle East seminar. The "barefoot doctor" approach of the Chinese
was attractive to many seminar participants as a way of reaching more
rural areas and creating a cadre of paramedical workers who would be
adequate, but not overtrained, for their tasks. In a similar vein there
was considerable interest in the African seminar in the self-help schemes
of Tanzania and Kenya, where strong efforts are under way to
recruit and train local people. In countries where village leaders operate
outside formal government structures, or where religious leaders make
authoritative statements on public issues and family behavior, special
efforts should be made to bring them into the processes of decision
making and policy implementation.

RELIGIOUS CONSTRAINTS

Any discussion of constituencies, the role of leaders, the political
forces affecting governments, and the cultural and moral elements surrounding the formulation and administration of population policies

must take account of religious teachings and beliefs and, above all, religious institutions.

Two major bodies of religious thought became the focus of seminar discussions: Roman Catholicism and Islam. The influence of the Roman Catholic Church was discussed at some length only in the Latin America–Commonwealth Caribbean seminar, and the role of Islam was examined in detail only in the Middle East seminar. Both religions have many adherents in Southeast Asia, but were discussed only briefly in that seminar. In neither the African nor the South Asian seminars did religion seem to preoccupy the participants, despite the prevalence of Islam in South Asia and in large parts of sub-Sahara Africa.

Although both religions have the appearance and reputation of exercising great influence on population matters, neither is a unified monolithic force. Participants said that the political influence of religious leaders on central governments is in some respects greater than their influence over the lives of individuals or couples. Neither religion interposes any obstacle to attempts to achieve reduction of morbidity or mortality; neither says anything about urbanization and internal migration; neither rejects the concept of "responsible parenthood" (see p. 48). Many who are religious practice family planning. In Latin American countries, for example, the incidence of abortion is high, suggesting that religious belief may have less of an impact on private behavior than has been thought.

Nonetheless, religion is likely to continue to affect the opinions that individuals express on public policies, and the church may win public support against abortion laws even among those who privately sanction abortions. Some seminar participants expressed the view that a frontal attack on existing laws is often politically unwise and that low-keyed programs may be politically more acceptable, such as the nonimplementation of laws prohibiting abortion, or the extension of family planning through the health services without an explicit public statement on fertility policy. Whether governments could then move incrementally to other population policies and programs without provoking powerful opposition from religious leaders and religious parties was unclear.

FOREIGN AID

Every seminar had a short but lively session on the problems that developing countries encounter in dealing with bilateral and multilateral aid agencies and, more specifically, with population-related public or private assistance. A preference for multilateral over bilateral aid was expressed; at the same time, several participants said that the paperwork required for both tends to become more and more alike and the need to fabricate goals and accomplishment rates is about the same for both.

It was commonly alleged that donor institutions fail to take sufficient account of differences among countries and the often highly individualized needs within countries. Moreover, many participants felt that the donor agencies are not always aware of the political costs, as well as benefits, that accompany foreign aid. Many deplored what they described as an overriding tendency of donor institutions to offer assistance for fertility limitation while simultaneously appearing to withhold assistance for health programs.

The more technically oriented participants often mentioned the usefulness of outside experts from international institutions. Their value ranged from helping to market the local experts' projects to actually providing much-needed technical advice and assistance. Foreign experts have been used to challenge each other or to challenge local forces to secure the rejection of certain activities or the acceptance of others.

On balance, it appears that the participants had a keen appreciation for the ways external assistance could help, a somewhat jaundiced view of the past history of foreign aid in the population field, and a willingness (in some cases a real plea) to continue working with the people who make foreign aid available. There was genuine appreciation for help that has made it possible for family-planning programs to get started, for research in contraception and reproductive biology, for training in demographic skills, and for the flexibility that donor institutions can display.

POLICY DIRECTIONS FOR THE FUTURE

Questions of population growth and distribution were seen at the national, community, family, and individual levels. An apparent point of consensus that did emerge was that national governments could and should use public policy to change demographic variables of their populations. Apart from this, however, there was great diversity of opinion on the types of policy instruments to use, the degree of coercion versus voluntary acceptance, and the objectives of population policies. It was clear that one country's policy today may be another country's option tomorrow, since the environment for policy formulation and execution differs widely from country to country.

A point in common was the widely shared concern over the distribution of people within countries. Urbanization and migration from rural to urban life worried pronatalists and antinatalists alike. Viewing the seminar participants as an indicative group leads one to conclude that a high priority for governments is the formulation of policy for internal population distribution and the discovery of ways to implement such policy.

Humanitarianism and the objectives of national development give the reduction of mortality and morbidity the highest priority in much of the developing world. It was also generally agreed that the reduction of infant and child mortality, in particular, would lower fertility, although the extent of the effect, its duration, and the time it would take were not established. The improvement of health conditions—sanitation, potable water, better food distribution, family health and nutrition education, and basic medical care in rural areas—was universally advocated by the seminar participants, as was the need for more effective policies and means to achieve them.

Controversy arose in each seminar—and sharp differences between regions were manifest—when discussion turned to policies to change the rate of population growth. Even the few participants who favored a pronatalist policy accepted the idea of "responsible parenthood" and the right of couples to decide the number of children they want, regardless of the decrees of "nature," "the state," or "ideology." Thus, one direction for the future may be popular rejection or reversal of policies that deny access to contraceptives and family-planning education. As couples become more aware of the possibility of planning or deciding their own future, they are likely to want to exercise their right of choice with respect to family size and insist that the state not restrict this right.

Even in pronatalist countries and others that are seemingly unconcerned with rapid population growth, governments are trying to cope with the results of rapid population growth that they perceive as undesirable—unemployment and underemployment, unplanned urbanization, squatter settlements, and despoiling land-use practices.

A large majority of the seminar participants believed it is incumbent on governments to take additional steps to reduce fertility. It was considered axiomatic that policy interventions devised for this purpose be consistent with, and preferably incorporated within, the overall development plan of the country. Fertility-reduction policies are never seen as a substitute for development policies. It was agreed that population variables have very direct effects on development plans and programs but that governments and public alike do not understand enough about the complex relationships between population growth and development. The greater this understanding is, the larger will be the constituency for fertility limitation.

The committee then perceived three major points of agreement on future policies:

1. There is a need for policies to deal with internal population distribution and effective means to implement them.

2. There is strong sentiment for better and more effective policies (and, by inference, expenditure) to reduce mortality and morbidity.

3. Regardless of a government's position on fertility, there must be policies and programs that are responsive to current existing problems created by rapid population growth.

The seminars revealed considerable support for social policies to achieve more equitable distributions of income and to improve the well-being of women and children. These policies are supported because they increase human welfare, but may receive additional support because they are assumed to have some effect on fertility, too, if accompanied by programs that foster the availability and knowledge of effective birth control measures. Such policies have the added attraction of fitting into a "balanced growth" approach, which draws on the interrelationship of policies to accelerate economic growth.

Many participants who did not support direct fertility-limiting policies favored measures to raise the age of marriage, limit or eliminate child labor, provide universal elementary education, and encourage women to enter the labor force. The expansion of educational and employment opportunities for women, it was argued, creates alternatives that are likely to result in a later age of marriage. In marriage, the alternative of work for wives outside the home may reduce the desire for large families. Greater expectations and opportunities for one's children result in greater costs in raising and educating each child, and, at the same time, diminish the productive contribution of the child to the household economy. The emergence of the nuclear, rather than the extended, family—greatly accelerated by industrial employment, urban housing, and increased spatial and occupational mobility—further reduces the economic productivity of children, particularly their function as old-age insurance. Through a variety of similar mechanisms, "modernization" shifts parental choices toward the small family.

Three issues must be clarified in each country, however, as future population-policy directions are charted:

1. The linkages between specific development measures and demographic variables must be identified and, if possible, their effects quantified.

2. A judgment must be made about the country's capacity to carry out the developmental policies that are regarded as desirable in themselves and that may also have an effect on population variables.

3. In each country a choice of priorities must be made with reference to resource constraints both human and material—to do more in any one field will tend to reduce the expenditure in some other field. But qualitative changes can often be made, for example, substitution of paramedical personnel for some highly trained physicians and greater emphasis on primary or vocational education instead of university education.

It was evident that, in the absence of hard data on the effectiveness (and on the secondary and tertiary effects) of most population policies, the seminar participants necessarily relied on common sense, empirical observations, philosophical predilections, ideological biases, and practical political considerations. That policy is made every day with inadequate data must not reduce the drive to acquire needed information. Almost all countries are conducting policy experiments in something close to a knowledge vacuum, but each seminar expressed the need for experimentation coupled with substantially greater analytical resources. Donor agencies were asked to back experimental policies and help assess their effectiveness, particularly in countries where fertility is regarded as a policy variable and where the governments do not simply adjust their aspirations to whatever fertility level happens to emerge as development proceeds.

The ways in which economic and social development interact with demographic variables are not well understood. But it is clear that no population policy can affect these variables in any country unless it has an impact on the human beings who have or will have children. In developing countries this is the great mass of the population—the urban and rural poor. Improvement in the conditions of life of the poor, their nutrition and health, their skills and opportunities, their access to information and understanding, their range of realizable aspirations may be an essential component of the process of transition from high to low mortality and fertility. Development policies with these objectives should be given much greater emphasis and a far greater share of resources than they have in the past.

ORDER FORM

A limited number of copies are available free to persons in the developing countries. A Spanish translation is planned for late 1974. Please type or print clearly on the labels below the name(s) of individuals, with their complete addresses, to whom you would like us to send a copy of *In Search of Population Policy: Views from the Developing World.*

For a Spanish copy print **SP** before the letter **A** on the label.

The label (s) should be returned to

Office of the Foreign Secretary
Commission on International Relations
National Academy of Sciences
2101 Constitution Avenue, N.W. (JH 204)
Washington, D.C., 20418 USA

A

A

A

A

A

A